NOT-FOR-PARENTS

The *Real*
WONDERS
of the
WORLD

WITHDRAWN

NOT-FOR-PARENTS

The Real WONDERS of the WORLD

MOIRA BUTTERFIELD

TIM COLLINS **ANNA CLAYBOURNE**

Lonely planet

Welcome to *Real* WONDERS

The world is a **wonderful planet** in ways you never imagined. Get ready for a world tour that no tourist has yet thought of. Visit a **crazy collection** of wondrous world locations that we've picked for their **WOW FACTOR** but also for their **WEIRDNESS FACTOR!**

They'll make you giggle, gasp, shake your head, stare, and start saying these words out loud every five minutes:

"LISTEN TO THIS!"

THIS WAY FOR THE CRAZIEST TOURIST TRIP EVER

CONTENTS

01

The highest, deepest, oldest, largest, longest, most famous, romantic, impressive, breathtaking, unusual, magical, expensive, mysterious, high-tech . . .

STUPENDOUS STRUCTURES

Burj Khalifa, p. 12

EMPIRE STATE BUILDING: TOWERS GET TALL

Building the world's tallest building has become a fierce competition among countries vying for the record, but it all began with New York's iconic Empire State landmark.

OLD-SCHOOL SKYSCRAPER

In 1931 New Yorkers were amazed to see the new Empire State Building, the first structure ever to have more than 100 floors. At 1,450 ft. (442 m) high, it was the world's tallest building for 40 years. In 1933 it starred in the world-famous movie *King Kong*, in a scene in which a giant monkey monster climbed to the top. The 102nd floor was originally designed as a landing platform for airships.

SKY RACE

Every year there is a footrace up 86 floors of the building, covering 1,576 stairs. The winning time is usually around 10 minutes.

WOW!

FACTS AND STATS FROM THE EMPIRE STATE

▶ The Empire State Building took just 13 months to build.

▶ Around 110 million people have visited it since it opened in 1931.

▶ It is struck by lightning around 100 times a year.

▶ Architects were told to design it to look like a young child's thick pencil.

MILE-HIGH MONSTER TOWER

The Empire State Building is small compared with more modern towers, and it will soon be even smaller. Kingdom Tower in Jiddah, Saudi Arabia, is planned for around 2025, and it will outstrip the current record holder, Burj Khalifa in Dubai (see p12). Nicknamed the "Mile High Tower," the new building is likely to stretch up a dizzying 5,250 ft. (1,600.2 m). Its upper part will have to be built by helicopter because no crane is tall enough.

TOP JOB

Reach high. Get a skyscraper window-cleaning job! Big buildings need constant outdoor cleaning, and skyscraper window polishers are more like mountaineers. They work on narrow platforms or dangling in seat cradles, clipped into safety harnesses. It's not a job for the fainthearted. In 2012 a window cleaner had to be rescued by firefighters from near the top of the 1,106-ft. (309.6-m) Shard building in London, England, when his cradle was caught in a strong wind gust and began swinging wildly.

WOW FACTOR

ONCE THE TOPMOST SECTION OF A SKYSCRAPER IS PUT IN PLACE, THE BUILDERS TRADITIONALLY HAVE A "TOPPING OUT" PARTY ON THE VERY TOP. THEY SOMETIMES EAT AN OPEN-AIR PICNIC WEARING THEIR SAFETY HARNESSES.

GOING UP

The Empire State Building's early skyscraper elevators don't compare to modern megatower ones, probably the closest experience to rocket travel on Earth. The fastest elevators zoom up at a top speed of around 3,313 ft. (1,010 m) a minute, roughly one floor every second. They are pressure controlled, so passengers don't get too much ear popping and stomach churning, and they are streamlined to cut down on vibration and noise.

GOING DOWN

Oil rigs stretch downward much farther than skyscrapers reach upward. The Magnolia Oil Platform in the Gulf of Mexico is the record holder, measuring 4,698 ft. (1,432 m) from its top to the seabed. It's not a building, though, because it doesn't support itself. It floats on the gulf surface anchored by giant steel tethers.

HIGHEST MEGATOWERS

Planned towers that will be higher than Burj Khalifa:

Kingdom Tower, Jiddah: 5,250 ft. (1,600 m)

Murjan Tower 1, Bahrain: 3,350 ft. (1,022 m)

Burj-Mubarak, Kuwait: 3,283 ft. (1,001 m)

Nakheel Tower, Dubai: 3,280 ft. (1000 m)

Towers that have already been built, in height order:

Burj Khalifa, Dubai: 2,717 ft. (828 m)

Abraj Al-Bait, Mecca: 1,971 ft. (601 m)

Shanghai World Financial Center, Shanghai: 1,614 ft. (492 m)

International Commerce Centre, Hong Kong: 1,588 ft. (484 m)

Petronas Towers, Kuala Lumpur: 1,483 ft. (452 m)

Taipei 101, Taipei: 1,338 ft. (408 m)

FEELING SKY SICK?

Tall skyscrapers are buffeted by strong winds, making them sway slightly at the top. The architects build in safety features called dampers to cut down on the swaying movement and stop people in the building from getting motion sickness. For instance, inside superskyscraper Taipei 101 there is a giant steel ball. As the building sways one way, the ball pushes in the other direction.

LOOK INSIDE!

At the very top, the tower sways back and forth by about 6.5 ft. (2 m) in high wind.

More than 22,000 glass panels.

57 elevators

BURJ KHALIFA:
WELCOME TO THE TOP

In 2010 Burj Khalifa in Dubai took the highest building record. At 2,717 ft. (828 m), it stretches up like a giant needle on the Dubai skyline and has been called the world's first superscraper. Anyone can take a trip to the top using a zooming elevator to see the breathtaking bird's-eye view from the highest observation deck on the planet.

SKYWARD

Burj Khalifa has the highest number of floors (163), the highest occupied floor, and the longest-distance elevator journey in the world, stretching up 1,653 ft. (504 m).

Gymnasium

WATER WORKING

Water vapor made in the building (by people breathing, for example) is automatically collected and sent to underground tanks for recycling in the gardens.

RECORD SWIM

Burj Khalifa opened with the world's highest swimming pool. Pool guests can swim in the sky, moving from the inside pool to an outside balcony.

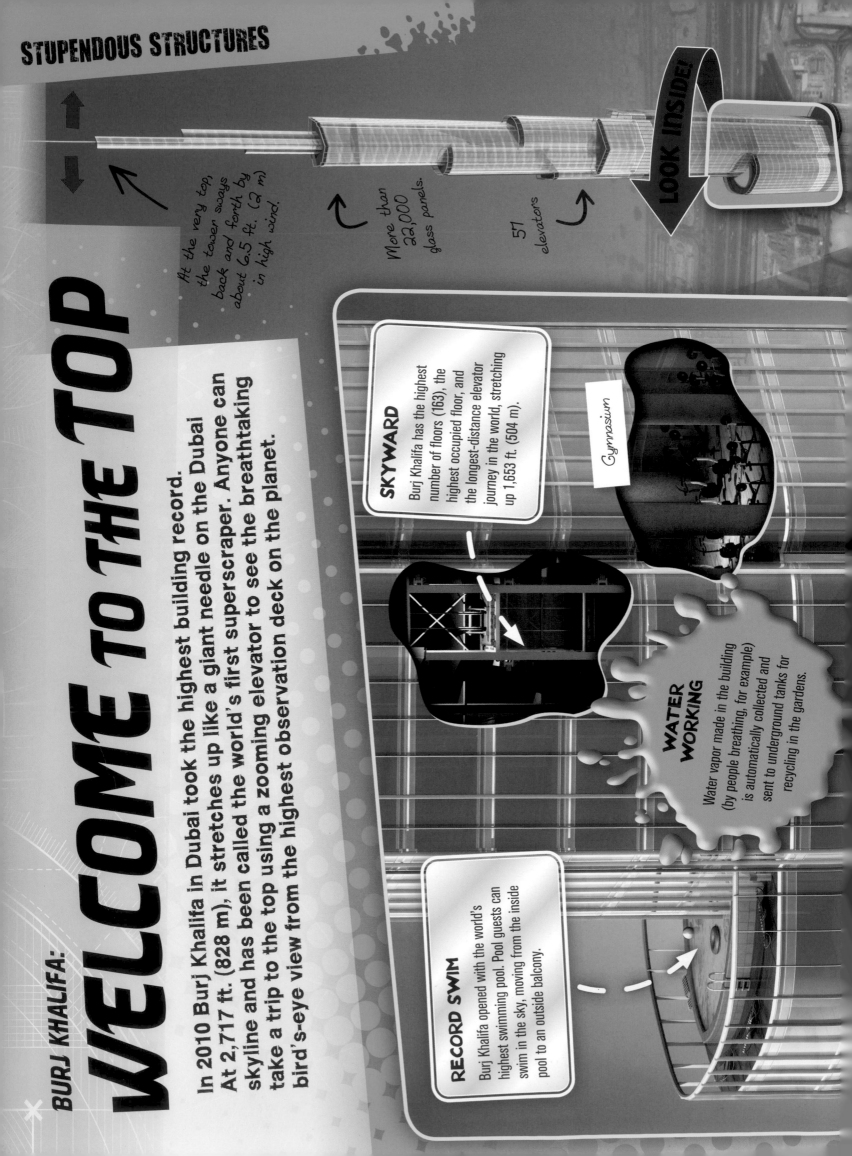

WOW FACTOR

US ARCHITECT ADRIAN D. SMITH GOT INSPIRATION FOR BURJ KHALIFA'S SHAPE FROM A HYMENOCALLIS, A TINY DESERT FLOWER. THE TOWER IS SHAPED IN THREE SECTIONS AROUND ITS CENTER, JUST LIKE THE FLOWER.

Burj Khalifa cost around $1 billion to build.

OOH!

Apartments

Offices

Shopping arcade

Restaurant

BUILDING THE BIG ONE

Burj Khalifa began with a huge foundation hole dug in the ground. One-hundred ninety-two enormous concrete-encased supporting piles were fitted in the hole to take the building's weight. The skyscraper was then gradually built upward using a framework of steel beams. The outside walls hang like curtains over the top of this super-strong steel skeleton.

STRONG STRUCTURE

Hidden behind the luxury rooms is a strong core of support columns and steel beams encased in concrete. Aluminum and stainless steel cladding covers the building, fitted with glass panels.

HIGH LIVING

Inside Burj Khalifa there are stores, a hotel, ultraluxury apartments, offices, and the world's highest restaurant, nightclub, and mosque.

STAR
STATUE OF LIBERTY

Statues are found all over the world, but few are as big and distinctive as the Liberty lady.

Statue of Liberty

Christ the Redeemer

Adult giraffe

LOOK AT THE SIZE OF THAT!

NATION'S PRIDE

The Statue of Liberty, in New York Harbor was a gift to the American people from France. It is made of 350 separate parts shipped from France in huge crates. They took nine years to fit together.

MAKING GIRAFFES LOOK SHORT

Some statues become instantly recognizable icons representing their country, and the Statue of Liberty is a good example. The statue of Christ the Redeemer in Rio de Janeiro, Brazil, is a similar symbol. To gauge how tall they are, imagine an adult giraffe. The Statue of Liberty is nearly 17 times taller, and Christ the Redeemer is more than 5 times taller than the giraffe.

STATUE OF LIBERTY STATS

▶ The statue was opened in 1886.

▶ The copper-skinned face is more than 8 ft. (2.4 m) high, and the waistline is 35 ft. (10.66 m) around.

▶ Total height with pedestal: 305.5 ft. (93 m). Without pedestal: 151 ft. (46.5 m) high.

▶ The seven giant crown rays represent seven continents.

▶ There are 154 steps inside the statue.

▶ The torch is covered in 24-carat gold leaf.

Web link
See the view from a webcam on the Statue of Liberty torch:
www.ellisisland.org/TorchCam/

JULY IV
MDCCLXXVI

Spring Temple

Mount Rushmore

HERE ARE SOME OTHER UNUSUAL GIANT STATUES:

01. Man meets the Sea–Esberg, Denmark.
02. Stone Buddha–Leshan, China.
03. A building pretending to be a statue–Fengdu, China.

RECORD BREAKERS

The world's tallest statue is the 419-ft. (128-m) gold-painted Spring Temple Buddha that sits on a hillside over Lushan, China. If you count its pedestal, it is 502 ft. (153 m) high–1.65 times higher than the Statue of Liberty. One of the world's biggest sculptures overall is on Mount Rushmore in South Dakota, where the heads of four US presidents are carved in the granite cliffs. The giant heads tower up to 59 ft. (18 m) tall, and each eye is around 11 ft. (3.35 m) wide.

BIG IN BRAZIL

The statue of Christ the Redeemer stands on a mountaintop above Rio de Janeiro. It is made of concrete and soapstone and reaches 119 ft. (36.1 m) high on its pedestal. Couples can marry in a chapel built underneath the statue.

What an Eiffel!

World-famous landmarks such as the Eiffel Tower still hold surprises . . .

Eiffel didn't design the tower. He bought the designs from another group of engineers.

The tower had a permit for twenty years and was then supposed to be torn down. Instead it was kept because it was useful as a radio mast.

At first many Paris architects and artists banded together to criticize the building, calling it "useless and monstrous."

LE TOWER

The 1,063-ft. (324-m) tall Eiffel Tower has come to symbolize Paris, the capital city of France. It was built in 1889 as an entrance arch for a world's fair, and it was named after engineering-firm owner Gustave Eiffel. It is one of the world's most popular monuments, with more than 7 million visitors yearly.

Small planes have flown beneath the tower through its arches.

WOW FACTOR

THE EIFFEL TOWER IS HELD TOGETHER BY 2.5 MILLION METAL RIVETS.

TOPPLING TOWER

Most people would recognize the Leaning Tower of Pisa, but did you know that it began to sink into the swampy ground beneath it before it was even finished? The name of the architect who originally designed the tower has been forgotten, but his mistake hasn't.

* The tower toppled further and further until 1990, when it was pulled back slightly and stabilized. Now it leans at an angle of 3.99 degrees.

* The Capital Gate Building in Abu Dhabi, United Arab Emirates, holds the record for the tower that leans the most. It was deliberately designed at an eighteen-degree angle.

PAINTING THE PIECES

The Eiffel Tower is repainted every seven years to stop the steel from rusting. Darker-colored paint is used at the bottom and lighter-colored paint is used at the top. It takes 25 painters 15 months and around 1,500 brushes to get the job done.

TEARDROP OF TIME

The Indian Taj Mahal is one of the best-known mausoleums (tomb buildings) in the world. It was built in the 1600s by ruler Shah Jahan in memory of his beloved third wife, Mumtaz Mahal. It was thought to be so beautiful that the poet Tagore called it "a teardrop on the cheek of time."

* An army of a thousand elephants did the heavy-lifting work on the Taj Mahal construction site.

* The gardens in front of the building are intended to represent Paradise.

Shah Jahan

HANDMADE ISLANDS

Check out this crazy collection of human-made islands dotted around the seas and lakes of the world.

Lake islands

CAREFUL WHERE YOU WALK

The Uros people live on more than 40 floating islands on Lake Titicaca between Bolivia and Peru. The islands are woven from the stalks of giant bulrushes. Walking on one of the islands is said to feel like walking on a water bed, and visitors must be careful not to put a foot through a thin section accidentally.

SHAPED FROM SAND

Dubai has two human-made island groups in the shape of palm trees (one is shown below) and a group of islands called "The World," built roughly in the shape of a world map. The Dubai islands are made of sand dredged up from the seabed.

Luxury mansions and hotels are built on Dubai's new islands.

Palm Islands

RECYCLE ISLAND

Richie Sowa has built his own island from more than 100,000 recycled plastic bottles stuffed into mesh bags and fishnets under wooden pallets. It is called Spiral Island 2, and it is tethered to the nearby shoreline of Mexico by rope. It even has its own swimming pool with a mini duck island in the middle.

Spiral Island 2

Flevoland

BUILT BIG

Flevoland in Holland is the world's biggest artificially-made island. It is land that was reclaimed from the sea by building dikes and pumping out millions of gallons of water. It is lower than sea level, so it has to be kept dry by constantly running electric drainage pumps.

Burj Al Arab

THE HEIGHT OF LUXURY

The world's first seven-star hotel, the Burj Al Arab, is built on an artificial island off the coast of Dubai, connected to the shore by a private bridge. The building is shaped like a giant sail, and 690 ft. (210 m) up it has a heliport that doubles as the world's highest tennis court.

THE ISLAND THAT WAS ART

Nowhere Island no longer exists, but for a while it was the world's newest nation. It was created by artist Alex Hartley from material excavated in the Arctic. It was towed around the coast of Great Britain during the 2012 London Olympics, and more than 23,000 people signed up to be its citizens. At the end of a year, they were each sent a piece of the island.

SUPREME STADIUMS

Modern sports stadiums are often impressive high-tech buildings, especially if they are connected to the Olympics.

The 2014 Sochi Winter Olympic stadium design was inspired by Russian jeweler Karl Fabergé, famous for his jeweled eggs.

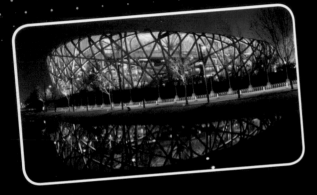

OLYMPIC GOLD

Each new Olympic Games needs several sports venues for all its events, but the grandest venue is usually the Olympic Stadium itself. In 2008 Beijing's Olympic Stadium (above) got the nickname the "Bird's Nest" because of its latticed shape. The organizers used traditional feng shui to plan the stadium position, believing it would bring peace and harmony to the games.

The London stadium during an Olympic ceremony.

OLYMPICS GOES GREEN

In the new millennium organizers are trying to make the Olympics more eco-friendly. The 2012 London Olympic Stadium was designed to be partly dismantled afterward, and it was surrounded by parkland for everyone to use after the games. The Olympic Village at the 2010 Vancouver Winter Olympics was heated with eco-friendly energy generated by sewage.

WOMEN OUT!

The first Olympics were held around 776 BC in ancient Greece, in an open-air stone stadium with religious temples attached. A crowd of around 40,000 spectators came to see the naked athletes, but married women were not allowed to attend. They risked death if they were caught watching.

The black-and-white pattern inside the London stadium.

SEATS OF POWER

The London Olympic Stadium seats were patterned black and white to create jagged lines that represented energy radiating from the track. By each seat there was a small lighting panel that was controlled by a central computer so the inside of the stadium could be spectacularly lit in different ways.

DREAM 2016

Rio de Janeiro, Brazil, hosts the Olympics in 2016, and this time the main stadium is so green, it's recycled! It is in an existing soccer stadium that is being updated. The Olympic Park is built on an old Formula One racetrack and juts out into a beautiful blue lagoon.

FLAME OF HISTORY

Each new Olympic Stadium has its own megatorch lit by a flame brought from Greece, birthplace of the first Olympics. The flame is transported from Greece by runners carrying a specially designed mini torch, such as the London torch on the right.

NEUSCHWANSTEIN: CRAZY CASTLE

Neuschwanstein in Bavaria, Germany, is one of the most impressive castles in the world, but the king who built it was impressively crazy!

Ludwig II was declared insane and was deposed before his castle was finished.

CUCKOO KING

King Ludwig II reigned in the 1800s but lived in his own fantasy world, imagining himself as a legendary medieval knight. He had Neuschwanstein Castle built as his hideaway and made it as medieval-looking as possible. He hated seeing people, so he stayed awake at night and slept during the day, and he was so eccentric that he even imagined he was having dinner with royal ghosts. Seven weeks after he died, his hideaway was opened to the public and has since had around 60 million visitors. That would really have made Ludwig mad!

I may have been crazy, but what a castle!

STATS & FACTS FROM NEUSCHWANSTEIN

▸ Ludwig's carved wooden bed took seventeen woodworkers 4.5 years to build.

▸ Watch out for the castle's appearance in the classic kid's movie *Chitty Chitty Bang Bang*.

▸ Ludwig had his own artificial cave built between his living room and his study, with a small waterfall and stalactites.

▸ There were plans for more than 200 rooms, but only 14 were completed and furnished by the time of Ludwig's death.

FAIRY-TALE FRENCH

French author Charles Perrault was inspired by chateaux (French castles) and the forests of France when he wrote some of the world's most famous fairy tales in the 1600s. For example, the Chateau Ussé inspired him to write *Sleeping Beauty*. He also wrote *Little Red Riding Hood* and *Cinderella*.

Chateau Ussé, fit for a princess

WOW FACTOR

CAN'T AFFORD YOUR OWN CASTLE TO LIVE IN? HOW ABOUT TRYING TO BEAT THE RECORD FOR THE WORLD'S TALLEST SAND CASTLE INSTEAD? IT CURRENTLY STANDS AT ALMOST 38 FT. (11.5 M) HIGH.

CASTLE OF THE LOST KING?

Ruined Tintagel Castle, on the coast of Cornwall, England, is said to be the site of the legendary King Arthur's court, but in reality nobody knows if Arthur really existed or where he was based. Today's ruins were first built in the 1200s by a nobleman who was probably a fan of the Arthur legends.

Ludwig's throne room, with no throne

Cartoon castle creator Walt Disney

SPOT WHAT'S MISSING

King Ludwig had the inside of his dream castle decorated with paintings of medieval legends. He spent a fortune on the decorations, including a sumptuous throne room, but he lost his job as king before his workers had time to put in a throne for him.

CASTLE CREATION

Neuschwanstein and other similar European castles inspired world-famous animator Walt Disney to create his design for Cinderella Castle.

ANZHAITE: BIG BRIDGE

The Anzhaite suspension bridge is one of the most awesome around.

1,102 FT. HIGH

TALLEST HANGING BRIDGE

The Anzhaite Long-Span Suspension Bridge, in Hunan, China, takes the record for the tallest suspension bridge held up by cables. It hangs 1,102 ft. (335.89 m) above Dehang Canyon. The photos on this spread show brave painters completing the bridge, one of them walking along with no harness!

LIT UP ABOVE

Anzhaite Bridge's 3,858 ft. (1,176m) span is lit by almost 2,000 bulbs at night. It links two road tunnels running through mountains on each side.

WOULD YOU WALK?

Brave walkers who aren't afraid of heights have their own safe walkway below the road on the Anzhaite Bridge (shown right). They get fantastic views of the spectacular forest-carpeted canyon far below.

NO DIY NEEDED

Old bridges need constant repainting and maintenance to keep them from rusting, but the latest bridges are made from material that needs to be treated much less frequently.

102 MI. LONG

OOH!

1,125 FT. HIGH

THE RECORD HOLDER

The Danyang-Kunshan Grand Bridge is the longest bridge in the world. It is a railroad viaduct stretching an incredible 102 mi. (164.8 km) between Beijing and Shanghai, China. It took four years to build and cost a hefty $8.5 billion.

TALLEST SUPPORTED BRIDGE

At 1,125 ft. (343 m) high, Millau Viaduct in France is the world's highest viaduct (a bridge supported by pillars). It carries a stretch of road between Paris and Montpellier.

Web link

There's a webcam on the Millau Viaduct, if you want to check out the dizzying view for yourself: www.lcviaducdemillau.com/en_index.php#/accueil/

TAU TONA: DEEP STUFF

BOOM!

To reach gold you've got to dig deep underground, find rocks containing gold, and blast them out. It is one of the world's most dangerous jobs, and it takes place in the world's deepest mine at Tau Tona, near Johannesburg, South Africa.

ROCK EXPLOSIONS

The tunnel walls of the mine can explode unexpectedly because of stresses on the rocks. To prevent this from happening, the rocks are sprayed with a mixture of concrete and steel fibers called shotcrete, held in place with netting.

QUAKE ZONE

The mine shafts at Tau Tona are so deep that earthquakes are a constant danger. Earthquake monitoring stations are dotted around the mine to give the workers an early warning of any tremors.

FEELING THE HEAT

Deep down under the surface of Earth, temperatures start to heat up. Without cooling systems the temperature in Tau Tona could reach up to a deadly 131°F (55°C). Mushy ice called "ice slurry" is pumped underground to keep the air temperature around 82°F (28°C), while giant fans on the surface keep air flowing through ventilation shafts into the tunnels.

FACTS FROM FAR BELOW

Stats & facts from Tau Tona

- At its deepest, the mine goes 2.4 mi. (3.9 km) down.
- There are around 500 mi. (800 km) of tunnels in the mine.
- The name Tau Tona means "great lion" in the Setswana language.
- It takes about an hour to reach the rock face from the surface in a cagelike elevator.

THE BUSINESS OF FINDING GOLD

Rocks are blasted out from the tunnel walls using handheld air drills or big drill rigs. The rocks are taken to the surface to be crushed into powder so that the gold can be separated out. Gold is weighed and sold by the ounce, and at Tau Tona each ton of rock provides around 0.35 oz. (9g) of gold. It costs approximately $550 to extract an ounce of gold from Tau Tona, and an ounce sells for around $1,300.

TOP TUNNELS

Road and rail tunnels are blasted out of rock, too. Here are three of the longest.

Longest road tunnel: Lærdal Tunnel, Norway: 15.23 mi. (24.5 km). Roughly a twenty-minute car drive from end to end.

Longest undersea tunnel: Seikan Tunnel, Japan: 33.46 mi. (53.85 km)—a railroad tunnel.

Longest tunnel overall: Gotthard Base Tunnel, Switzerland: 35.4 mi. (57 km) long—a railroad tunnel.

▶ AN EASIER WAY

In the 1800s thousands of people went to California to take part in the gold rush, hoping to find valuable gold nuggets. They panned for gold, using a sieve to try to separate out small gold pieces from the rock debris in streams. You can still try gold panning for yourself in some of California's National Parks and in other gold-rich spots around the world. Happy nugget hunting!

Gold-panning equipment

GIZA: THE GREAT PYRAMID PUZZLE

For thousands of years the Great Pyramid of Giza was the tallest structure in the world, but it was built for only one man. It was designed as a tomb for the ancient Egyptian pharaoh Khufu, who died around 2500 BC, but there's something weird about this burial place. Inside there are burial chambers, tunnels, and air shafts, but no body has yet been found . . .

Pyramid of Menkaure, Khufu's grandson

2.3 MILLION BLOCKS!

More than 2.3 million building blocks were used to build Khufu's pyramid. It took around 20 years.

The ancient Egyptians often buried animal mummies, including snakes, cats, dogs, crocodiles, and falcons, along with humans, but not in the Great Pyramid.

sSSs!

PYRAMID SECRETS

- There are three large pyramids at Giza (shown below), plus other tombs and boat pits, where full-size wooden boats were buried for use in the afterlife.

- In the 1800s excavators found a mummy coffin in the smallest Giza pyramid and sent it to England by ship, but the ship sank.

- In ancient Egyptian myth Pharaoh Khufu consulted a magician called Djedi while building his pyramid.

- There are three chambers in Khufu's pyramid: the King's Chamber, the Queen's Chamber, and an unfinished mystery chamber.

- The Great Sphinx statue sits in front of the Great Pyramid. It shows Khufu as a half-lion, half-man god.

- The Great Sphinx's nose has been knocked off. For years Napoleon's troops were blamed for doing it in the 1700s, but the nose had come off long before that date.

- Nobody knows where Khufu is really buried. It's possible that he could still be in a hidden part of the pyramid.

- It is possible that the pyramid could have been built to represent the rays of the Sun streaming down from the heavens.

Great Sphinx

WHERE DID KHUFU GO?

Inside the Great Pyramid some of the tunnels are aligned with (pointing at) important stars. It is thought that the builders may have believed that Khufu's soul would travel up these tunnels to the heavens. In the main chamber there is a big stone tomb, but nobody knows why there is no preserved body and no treasure. Other Egyptian tombs are packed with valuable goods for the dead to take with them on their journey to the afterlife.

Pyramid of Khafre, Khufu's son

Great Pyramid of Khufu

STAR TUNNELS

Some mysterious narrow tunnels in the Great Pyramid are blocked by stone walls. Work is going on to explore them using a snake-shaped robot equipped with a tiny camera. It is possible that they lead nowhere and were designed as magical pathways for the pharaoh in the afterlife.

Scarab beetle amulets (carvings) were sacred to ancient Egyptians. They were placed on top of the hearts of mummified bodies, but not in the Great Pyramid.

02

The best of the best, the most luxurious, the yummiest, the most expensive, and the wackiest top treats in the world? It's . . .

THE GOOD LIFE

Hydropolis Hotel, Dubai, p. 33

NICE 'N' ICY ICEHOTEL

Would you like to stay somewhere a little different? At the Icehotel in Jukkasjärvi, Sweden, you can sleep on a bed made of ice. Or perhaps you might prefer to sleep in a hotel underwater or up a tree!

WARM WELCOME, COLD BEDS

The Icehotel melts every spring and gets rebuilt each winter to a new design. It has ice bedrooms (see right), an ice bar, and even an ice chapel. All of the furniture is carved from ice, but the toilets are not.

THE INSIDE OF THE ICEHOTEL STAYS AT A CONSTANT COLD TEMPERATURE OF ABOUT 28°F (−5°C), SO GUESTS MUST WRAP UP WARMLY.

In the hotel's ice bar the glasses are made of ice, and guests must wear gloves to hold them.

ON LOAN FROM THE RIVER

The hotel is made of ice taken from the local Torne River when it is frozen. Instead of cement, the blocks are held together by snice, a sprayed-on cross between snow and ice.

SLEEP WITH THE FISHES

If ice doesn't sound nice, how about staying in this underwater hotel being planned off the coast of Dubai, United Arab Emirates? Hydropolis will have a hotel above water linked by pillars to bedrooms 32 ft. (10 m) down below the sea surface.

Weddings are held in an ice chapel at the Swedish Icehotel.

CREATIVE COOL

Artists create amazing ice art for the Icehotel. Sculptures have included chandeliers, ice dogs, polar bears, and even an ice goldfish bowl with an ice fish inside.

This Icehotel room had a snowflake art theme.

TOP TREE HOUSES

The Treehotel is another unusual place to stay in Sweden. It is made up of designer tree houses perched in the branches of a snowy forest. There's a log-cabin tree house, a room that looks like a giant bird's nest, and even one that is shaped and lit up to look like a UFO (left).

CAVES OF CAPPADOCIA

The region of Cappadocia in Turkey can claim to have more hidden homes than anywhere else in the world. Check out the cave cities there and discover some other unusual addresses, too.

DIG IT

For around 2,000 years, local people have been hollowing out the soft rock of the Cappadocian landscape to make secret cave homes where they could hide from invaders.

STREETS OF STONE

Gradually the cave homes were linked by underground passages, creating narrow streets. Many underground villages developed, some stretching up to eight stories high in the rock. More than a thousand churches were carved from the rock, too.

People still live in the caves. You can stay in guest cave rooms and visit the cave churches, such as this one, called Karanlik.

ENEMIES NOT INVITED

The cave dwellers built in cunning home security systems to defend themselves against enemy visitors. They could roll massive stones across entrances to block the way or throw spears down through holes dug in passageway ceilings.

SEAWEED STYLE

Spanish architect Antoni Gaudi's homes use the natural world, but in a different way from the cave homes. Gaudi used curved stonework and twisted iron to imitate nature. You can visit some of the buildings he designed in the 1800s in the city of Barcelona, Spain.

Gaudi's Casa Batló building (left) was inspired by the colors and shapes of sea coral.

A colorful chimney on a Gaudi home

CRAZY CRIB

Don't want to live underground? How about upside down? In 2012 builders made an upside-down house in Austria, together with upside-down rooms and an upside-down car in the garage. It is open as a tourist attraction.

A room in a Turkish cave

BUCKINGHAM PALACE:
SECRETS OF THE PALACE

If you think your home is roomy, wait until you see London's Buckingham Palace, the official home of the British monarch. Most of the palace is private, but there's nothing to stop you from exploring your very own royal cross-section.

The Music Room, where royal babies are christened

The Picture Gallery, displaying fine art such as works by Leonardo da Vinci and Rembrandt

SHE'S IN

When Queen Elizabeth is in the palace, the sovereign's flag flies above the entrance. The queen and Prince Philip have their own private rooms in the north wing. Every morning a bagpiper plays under the queen's private window at 9:00 a.m.

PALACE STATS

- 19 state rooms
- 240 bedrooms
- 8 bathrooms
- 92 offices
- More than 40,000 light bulbs
- 760 windows (cleaned every six weeks)
- More than 20,000 works of art
- Building dates from 1825 onward.
- The queen has her own post office and a private cinema.
- There is a heliport, a lake, and a tennis court in the gardens.

The Grand Staircase

VISITORS THIS WAY!

The public state rooms are in the west wing. Banquets are held there, with dinner served on golden plates. In one year alone, the queen entertains more than 50,000 guests at dinners, receptions, and garden parties.

LOOK INSIDE!

West wing

Queen's Private Entrance

Ambassadors' Entrance

Front Entrance facing the Mall

Gardens this way

Private swimming pool

WOW FACTOR

THE QUEEN HAS HER OWN ROYAL MEWS, WHERE HER OFFICIAL COACHES, OR CARRIAGES, ARE KEPT. THEY INCLUDE THE GOLD STATE COACH (RIGHT), WHICH IS PULLED BY EIGHT HORSES.

PEOPLE INSIDE

Around 450 people work in the palace, including cooks, cleaners, gardeners, and the monarch's personal waiting staff. There are even two people who take care of more than 350 clocks.

The Throne Room

WOW!

ON GUARD

Foot guards patrol outside, wearing red jackets and tall bearskin hats. Mounted guards are on patrol, too. When new guards come on duty each day, there is a ceremony called "Changing the Guard" held near the palace. Every morning the gravel on the forecourt of the palace is cleaned and combed by machine to make it look perfect.

Grand Entrance

Web link

Find out more about Buckingham Palace at www.royal.gov.uk/ TheRoyalResidences/ Buckingham Palace/ BuckinghamPalace.aspx

DUBAI MEGAMALL

The Dubai Mall has some surprises for its shoppers. Find out why it's made such a big splash and discover some of the world's other big shopping hot spots.

SHOP WITH SHARKS

The Dubai Mall is one of the biggest in the world, and it has the planet's biggest suspended aquarium tank, filled with more than 20 million gallons (10 million liters) of water. Around 33,000 sea creatures live inside, including many tiger sharks and stingrays.

WOW FACTOR

THE DUBAI MALL AQUARIUM SPRANG A LEAK IN 2010, PANICKING SCARED SHOPPERS. FROGMEN DIVED IN TO REPAIR IT.

STATS AND FACTS FROM THE DUBAI MALL

- The mall has a giant indoor waterfall.
- It has more than 160 restaurants and an indoor theme park.
- You can view the aquarium creatures from a glass-bottom boat or even swim with them.
- The mall began by covering 12 million sq. ft. (1.1 million sq m), but it is growing.

You can take a submarine ride at West Edmonton Mall.

SHOP AND SWIM

Another watery shopping spot is West Edmonton Mall in Alberta, Canada, the largest mall in North America. As well as 800 stores, an ice-skating rink, and a glow-in-the-dark miniature golf course, it has the world's largest indoor water park and the world's tallest indoor bungee-jumping tower.

WINTER WONDERLAND

The super-sized Mall of the Emirates in Dubai is home to Ski Dubai–the Middle East's first indoor ski center. Featuring five slopes, a black run, toboggan courses, ice caves, an ice slide, and giant snowballs, the ski center also has its very own penguins who come out to play each day.

SHOP 'TIL YOU DROP

The Khan Shatyr Shopping Mall in Astana, Kazakhstan, is covered by the world's largest tent.

The New South China Mall in Dongguan, China, is the world's biggest mall, with room for 2,350 stores. However, many of them are empty.

The busiest mall in the world is the Mall of America in Bloomington, Minnesota, with around 42 million visitors a year.

Here's a bedazzling bagful of shopping malls with some special claims to fame.

The Villagio Mall in Doha, Qatar, has a fake sky that changes colors above the heads of the shoppers walking below.

BIG IN THE BIG APPLE

FAO Schwartz in New York is the oldest toy shop in the United States and is famous for its giant floor piano (below), which featured in the movie *Big*. It also sells luxury toys, such as a jewel-encrusted Etch A Sketch worth $1,500 and a foosball table costing $25,000.

Deyrolle: WORLD'S WEIRDEST STORE

Do you have a stuffed dead animal on your shopping list? That's no problem at the world's freakiest, most far-out store.

OOH!

STUFFED STORE

The Deyrolle taxidermy store has been in Paris since 1831 as the go-to destination for anyone wanting to buy a stuffed dead animal or to get their beloved dead pet made lifelike again. All sorts of stuffed creatures are sold there, including full-size animals wearing human clothing.

YOU CAN RENT STUFFED ANIMALS FROM DEYROLLE FOR PARTIES!

BUY SOME LUCK

Another animal shopping stop is the Witch's Market in La Paz, Bolivia, where local people buy their good-luck charms. Many Bolivians believe that burying a dried baby llama (left) under their home will bring good luck. A dried frog will bring money, and a dried armadillo will stop thieves from visiting.

A Witch's Market buy

FREAKY FACTS FROM DEYROLLE

▸ At Deyrolle any animal can be stuffed, but the shop has refused requests by humans to have themselves stuffed after death.

▸ Most customers tend to buy the rocks, fossils, and small insect displays sold at Deyrolle, rather than big creatures such as lions and polar bears.

MAGIC MARKET

The Voodoo Market at Lome in Togo, Africa, may be an even weirder shopping experience than Deyrolle. It sells ingredients used by local witch doctors, so the market stalls (below) are piled with animal body parts, bones, and protective magical statues.

Deyrolle has many abandoned pet cats and dogs that were brought in by their owners for stuffing and then never collected.

ROBOT RESTAURANT

China's Robot Restaurant takes the cake for being wonderfully weird.

METAL MEAL

At the Robot Restaurant in Harbin, 20 robots greet, serve, and even cook the food. At the door a robot usher greets customers with the words "Earth person, hello."

WOW FACTOR

THE HARBIN ROBOTS ARE WORTH AROUND $40,000 EACH AND CAN MAKE 10 DIFFERENT FACIAL EXPRESSIONS.

ROBOT RECHARGE

Robots cook dumplings and noodles and serve them by running along tracks around the tables. Every five hours a robot needs a meal of its own—a two-hour recharge of electricity.

At the Pay as You Please café in Ireland you can pay as much as you believe your meal was worth.

At pet cafés in Japan customers can cuddle cute creatures such as cats and rabbits when they visit.

At Al Johnson's Swedish Restaurant in Sister Bay, Wisconsin, goats graze on the restaurant's grass roof.

In the Japan Grillhaus in Austria customers get fined if they leave anything on their plate at the end of the meal.

At the Ka-Tron Flying Chicken in Thailand, barbecued chickens are set on fire and catapulted through the air to be caught by waiters on unicycles.

Guests at Isdaan in the Philippines are encouraged to release their pent-up anger by shouting and throwing cups, plates, and even TVs at a special wall.

EAT THIS!

Here are some other crazy snack spots for adventurous food explorers who want to eat their way around the world.

EATING IN THE DARK

A number of restaurants around the world now offer eating in complete darkness. Diners must concentrate on the taste and smell of the food alone, not the way it looks.

Waiters wear night-vision goggles at the Dark Restaurant in Beijing, China.

"Dining in the Sky" over Beirut and Berlin.

PIE IN THE SKY

"Dining in the Sky" is on offer for anyone in the world who wants to pay for a 22-person dinner table, plus a chef, waiter, and entertainer, to be hoisted 164 ft. (50 m) in the air by crane. The diners get strapped into their seats, but they might need to cross their legs because there is no bathroom.

Tasty Science

Save up to try one of the super-luxury restaurants judged to be among the best in the world. But only consider it if you like trying new things . . . REALLY new things!

LISTEN, SMELL, AND LICK

British chef Heston Blumenthal is world-famous for using science to make unique new foods. He is interested in the way food sounds, smells, and feels, as well as how it tastes. He might experiment to make a dish sound more crunchy when it is eaten, for instance. If guests at his Fat Duck restaurant in England order Sound of the Sea (below), they will find themselves listening to ocean noises on an iPod hidden inside a conch shell while eating different kinds of fish and seaweed, as well as sea jelly beans and edible "sand."

Heston Blumenthal's most famous dishes include snail porridge and egg-and-bacon ice cream (above).

These shimmering, tiny jelly-like fingers were El Bulli's unique version of grilled vegetables.

Ravioles, tiny spheres of tasty gel created in a food lab.

SPANISH STYLE

El Bulli in San Sebastian, Spain, won a record number of Michelin Stars, an award given to top restaurants every year. It made chef Ferran Adrià famous as arguably the world's best chef. His unique food inventions included such unusual choices as a frozen cheese balloon, parmesan frozen air with muesli, a beet-and-yogurt meringue, and an air baguette. Ferran Adrià has influenced many chefs around the globe and, instead of running a restaurant, he has now decided to set up a "think tank" to invent entirely new food flavors that cooks around the world will use.

MUNCHING THE COUNTRYSIDE

Noma in Copenhagen, Denmark, is judged by many to be the world's best restaurant. The chef, René Redzepi, bases his food on foraging—cooking with things that he finds in the countryside. His dishes include a flowerpot of vegetables and flowers in an "edible soil," sea urchin toast, and live red ants with crème fraîche (diners say they taste like lemongrass).

A Noma dish, beautifully served, made up of many different flavors carefully put together.

TASTY SCIENCE

Chefs such as Heston Blumenthal and Ferran Adrià use a style of cooking that is sometimes called molecular gastronomy. They use science to reinvent food tastes, colors, and shapes, creating new dishes by experimenting with scientific laboratory equipment. They might create scented air for a diner to sniff, flavored powders, and capsules filled with taste gel. The idea is for the diner to have fun as well as taste good things, and dishes cooked in this way often sound crazy but taste wonderful.

CHUTTERS: The Sweet Spot

Check out candy paradise Chutters and some other candylicious locations that have yummy candies and ice creams licked. Enjoy!

CHUTTERS

The New Hampshire candy store Chutters has the world's longest candy counter (shown below). Its line of sweet-treat-stuffed jars stretch for an amazing 112 ft. (34 m).

CHOOSING AT CHUTTERS

Chutters' record-breaking three-tiered candy counter holds around 800 candy jars. Some are nostalgic candies, the kind your grandma ate. Others are rare flavors and brands or tooth-friendly sugar-free varieties.

YUM!

M&M'S WORLD

This glitzy Las Vegas store beats Chutters for sheer candy numbers. It has four whole floors of M&M's products to buy (shown left).

CANDYLICIOUS

The giant Candylicious store in Dubai is the biggest candy store in the world, with 10,000 sq. ft. (1,000 sq m) of sugary shop treats. It even has a giant lollipop tree.

DYLAN'S CANDY BAR

This stylish New York store calls itself a designer sweet boutique. It stocks around 7,000 candy treats brought from around the world.

ICE CREAM CITY

This Tokyo ice cream park has hundreds of flavors for sale, some of them very strange. Soy chicken, orchid root, or eel ice cream anyone? Yes, that reads *eel ice cream!*

PAPABUBBLE

At Papabubble stores around the world you can watch designer candy being handmade daily. Papabubble's special delicacies include giant caramel toothbrushes (but don't tell your dentist).

JELLY BELLY UNIVERSITY

In Fairfield, California, you can go to Jelly Belly University at the Jelly Belly Candy Company. You can spend a day learning all about how to make delicious jelly beans and graduate with a degree in beanology.

HERSHEYPARK

The town of Hershey, Pennsylvania, is the home of the Hershey Chocolate Company. It offers chocolate fans a chocolate-themed amusement park and even chocolate spa treatments.

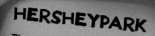

03

The fastest, highest, longest, craziest, riskiest, funniest, most exciting, breathtaking, magical, glamorous, dangerous . . .

THRILLS, SPILLS, AND GAMES

Top roller-coaster rides, p. 52

THRILLS, SPILLS, AND GAMES

FABULOUS BRICKS

Imagine a terrific tour of the planet's greatest theme parks, starting with one made from millions of tiny bricks.

MINI MILLIONS

LEGOLAND® in Billund, Denmark, is right next to the factory where LEGO® bricks are made. It has roller coasters, water rides, and themed games, but perhaps the most famous part of the park is Miniland, which features models of world landmarks built using more than 25 million LEGO bricks. Part of London, England, is shown right. LEGOLAND theme parks can be found in other countries, too.

Full-time modelmakers build the LEGOLAND constructions, which must be one of the world's coolest jobs. The models are planned on a computer first.

IT'S A WINNER

The Golden Ticket Award is an Oscar-style ceremony for the world's theme parks, and for fifteen years Cedar Point in Ohio has won "Best Amusement Park." It has 72 rides and bills itself as the "roller-coaster capital of the world."

The Wicked Twister at Cedar Point.

LEGOLAND HOLIDAYS

WOW FACTOR

A BRITISH MAN WAS SUCH A BIG FAN OF THE LEGOLAND® WINDSOR RESORT, ENGLAND, HE CHANGED HIS NAME TO "LEGOLAND WINDSOR."

LEGO STATS AND FACTS
- LEGO is made up of two Danish words meaning "play well."
- There are more than 58 million LEGO bricks in the Billund park.
- A tower of 40,000 million LEGO bricks would reach the Moon.

This giant shark won't bite because it's made of LEGO.

DISNEY STYLE

Perhaps the most famous theme park in the world is Disneyland, opened in California in 1955. Some of the park's rides have even been made into movies. *Pirates of the Caribbean, The Haunted Mansion, The Tower of Terror,* and *Mission to Mars* were all Disney theme-park rides before they became hit movies.

There are now Disneylands around the world.

Pirates of the Caribbean

Dollywood in Tennessee: Country singer Dolly Parton's Dolly-based theme park, with her own interactive museum.

Suoi Ten Amusement Park in Vietnam: A Buddhist-themed water park created to simulate the Buddhist idea of heaven.

CRAZY BUT COOL

Here are some other theme parks with a difference:

World Chocolate Wonderland in Beijing, China: The world's largest chocolate replica of the Great Wall of China.

Crocosaurus Cove in Darwin, Australia: A croc-themed park where you can go into the Cage of Death, a see-through underwater cage in a croc-infested tank.

WHITE KNUCKLE RIDES

Many theme parks have claimed to have the world's greatest roller coaster. But which one really leads the way for heart-in-the-mouth excitement?

KINGDA KA

The Kingda Ka roller coaster in Six Flags Great Adventure in New Jersey is the world's tallest roller coaster, at 456 ft. (139 m). It takes just 3.5 seconds to get up to a screamingly fast speed of 128 mph (206 kph)!

STATS AND FACTS FROM KINGDA KA

- The jungle-themed ride is named after a mythical tiger. A real Bengal tiger once lived on the site next to the ride.

- The ride climbs up to the top of the main tower, 456 ft. (139 m) high, before plunging downward through a steep spiral.

- People under 4 ft. 7 in. (1.4 m) can't go on Kingda Ka, but they don't have to miss out. You can experience movies of the ride on YouTube.

FORMULA ROSSA

Formula Rossa, at Ferrari World in the United Arab Emirates, is the world's fastest roller coaster, with a top speed of 150 mph (241 kph). It is so fast that anyone who rides it has to wear safety goggles to protect their eyes.

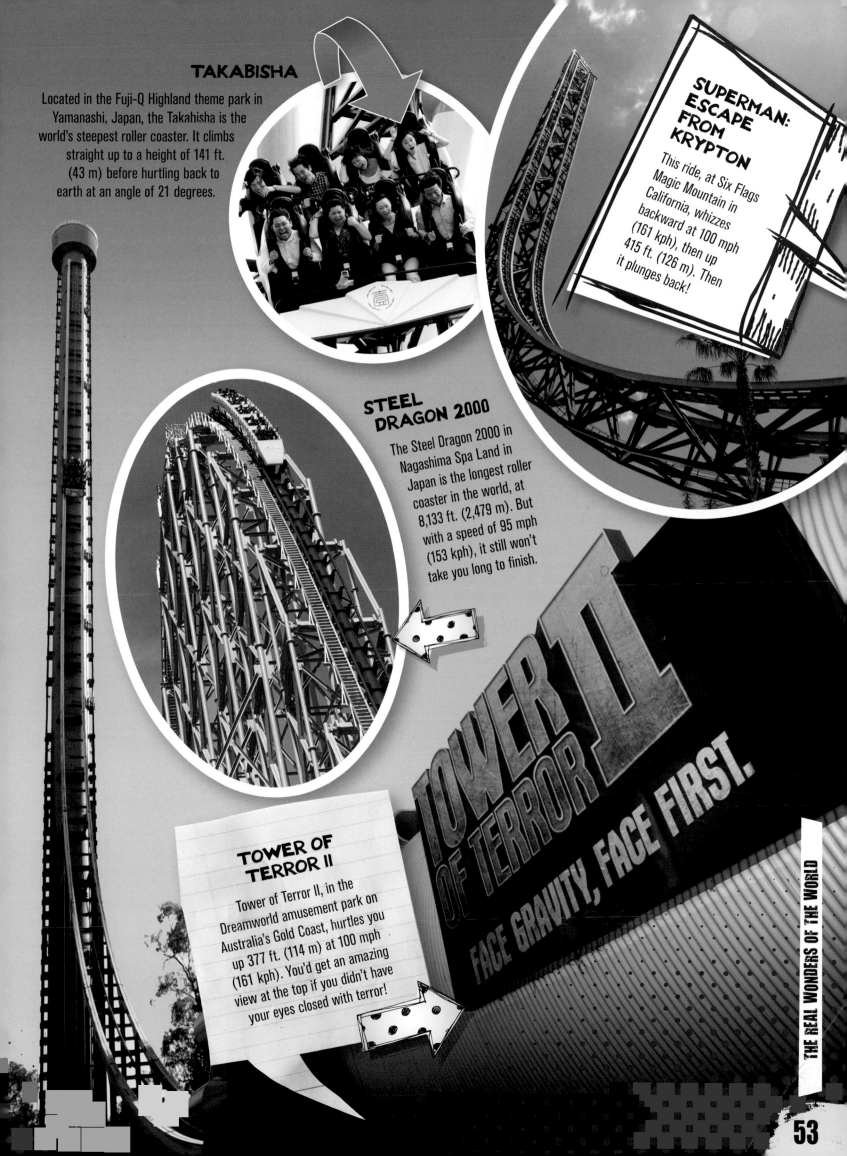

TAKABISHA

Located in the Fuji-Q Highland theme park in Yamanashi, Japan, the Takahisha is the world's steepest roller coaster. It climbs straight up to a height of 141 ft. (43 m) before hurtling back to earth at an angle of 21 degrees.

SUPERMAN: ESCAPE FROM KRYPTON

This ride, at Six Flags Magic Mountain in California, whizzes backward at 100 mph (161 kph), then up 415 ft. (126 m). Then it plunges back!

STEEL DRAGON 2000

The Steel Dragon 2000 in Nagashima Spa Land in Japan is the longest roller coaster in the world, at 8,133 ft. (2,479 m). But with a speed of 95 mph (153 kph), it still won't take you long to finish.

TOWER OF TERROR II

Tower of Terror II, in the Dreamworld amusement park on Australia's Gold Coast, hurtles you up 377 ft. (114 m) at 100 mph (161 kph). You'd get an amazing view at the top if you didn't have your eyes closed with terror!

TOWER II OF TERROR

FACE GRAVITY, FACE FIRST.

KJERAG, NORWAY: HIGH in the SKY

Don't have a head for heights? Then you'd better avoid this hot spot for height-loving thrill seekers.

WATCH OUT BELOW

Watch out for falling people if you're walking in the mountains of Kjerag in Rogaland County, Norway! The steep mountainsides are a favorite spot for BASE jumping, an extreme sport in which you jump from a great height and use a parachute to break your fall. Thousands jump from the high cliffs every year.

AAAGH!

STATS AND FACTS FROM KJERAG

- BASE jumpers plummet 3,228 ft. (984 m) down the cliffs at Kjerag.

- Around 3,000 people a year try jumping from the cliff tops.

- Kjerag has a famous boulder, the Kjeragbolten, wedged high up between two steep cliff faces. People climb up to stand on the boulder.

WOW FACTOR

BASE STANDS FOR "BUILDINGS, ANTENNAE, SPANS, AND EARTH"— A LIST OF THE FIXED SURFACES YOU CAN JUMP FROM. SPANS MEANS BRIDGES, AND EARTH MEANS CLIFFS.

BASE jumping is one of the world's most dangerous sports. Unfortunately, there are regular fatal accidents.

TOUGHEST TO THE TOP

Jumping needs bravery, but climbing requires a lot of strength and concentration. One of the most challenging climbing sites of all is El Capitan in Yosemite National Park in California. Its rock face is incredibly smooth and almost vertical, and it was once considered impossible to climb. It was finally conquered in 1958.

ZIP DIP

Zip-lining is a much safer way to travel down, using a cable on a metal pulley. One of the world's steepest and longest zip lines is the ZipFlyer in Nepal, which is 5,905 ft. (1,800 m) long and plunges over a dense forest at 100 mph (161 kph).

WINGING IT

Lake Elsinore in California is a popular location for people flying in wing suits—a kind of all-in-one bodychute that slows down the wearer's falling speed. Wingsuits are also known as "flying squirrel suits."

READY, SETS, GO!

In the movie Mission Impossible: Ghost Protocol, Tom Cruise climbed up the outside of Dubai superscraper Burj Khalifa for real, with no stunt double.

CITY SPIDERMAN

In recent years some climbers have set their sights on human-made structures such as skyscrapers. Alain Robert from France has been branded the "real-life Spiderman" for scaling many prominent buildings, often without any equipment. In 2011 he scaled Burj Khalifa in just six hours.

Swamp Sports

Prepare yourself for swamp soccer and other muddy—or just plain crazy—sports events that you can win weirdly around the world.

IT'S A DIRTY GAME

Swamp soccer never gets called off because of waterlogged fields. It is played on deliberately flooded fields or in muddy bogs. The Swamp Soccer World Championships are held in Hyrynsalmi, Finland, every year, and hundreds of teams compete.

If you like the idea of mud but don't want to join a team, try the World Bog Snorkeling Championship, held in Wales, UK, every August. Competitors swim through a muddy, water-filled trench using flippers but not their arms.

For true game grime, go to Hamburg, Germany, for the European Mud Olympics. The down-and-dirty events include mud volleyball, mud tug-of-war, fish tennis, and an eel relay race using fake eels made of tire inner tubes filled with rotting fish.

Toe Wrestling: Contestants link their toes together and try to push their opponent's foot over. The world championships are held in Derbyshire, England.

Scenario Paintball: The Skirmish Invasion of Normandy is an annual US event in which more than 4,000 paintball players recreate a battle from World War II.

Cheese Rolling: Competitors chase a large cheese wheel down a very steep hill in this annual British contest. An ambulance and paramedics wait at the bottom.

Wife Carrying: The World Wife-Carrying Championships are held in Sonkajärvi, Finland, every year. Male contestants have to carry their wives around an obstacle course (left). The winner gets his wife's weight in beer.

SPORTS GONE NUTS

Yes, these events really do happen!

MUDDY MONEY

The European Mud Olympics raises a lot of money for charity, as well as being great fun for mud fans. It doesn't take place in a stadium. Instead competitors run around mudflats at the mouth of the Elbe River in Germany. In addition to sports medals, there are prizes for the funniest team name and the best fans.

SPLAT SPORT

Georgia is the yearly venue for the Summer Redneck Games. Contestants can enter for events such as the Mud Pit Belly Flop, where the winner is the one who makes the biggest mud splash. There is also a seed-spitting contest, toilet-seat throwing, and an armpit serenade competition.

Hooray for HOLLYWOOD

Hollywood, California, is the center of the American movie industry, and the Universal Studios Tour in Hollywood is one of the world's most famous behind-the-scenes movie studio tours.

Shrek appears at a Halloween carnival on the back lot at Universal Studios.

WOW!

Jurassic Park–The Ride: Based on the 1993 blockbuster *Jurassic Park*. Visitors travel on a raft past escaped dinosaurs trying to sabotage the ride. It ends with an 85-ft. (26-m) plunge into water.

King Kong 360 3-D: A huge, curved movie screen surrounds the studio tour tram, which shakes as those on board watch a 3-D battle between dinosaurs and monster ape King Kong.

TOP RIDES

Here are some of the top attractions at Universal Studios.

Web link
Check out all the different tours to take you behind the scenes: www.universalstudios hollywood.com/attractions/studio-tour/

The Studio Tour: Tours of famous movie sets, plus thrilling special effects such as a car chase, explosions from *The Fast and the Furious*, and a plane crash from *War of the Worlds*.

SIGN OF THE STARS

The word Hollywood is written in giant white letters on the mountains overlooking the district. The sign was put up in 1923 to advertise a housing development and originally spelled Hollywoodland.

READY, SETS, GO!

Six Hollywood studios are referred to as "majors" because they account for around 90% of box office takings between them. The list includes Columbia Pictures, Warner Bros., Walt Disney, Universal, Fox, and Paramount Pictures.

WALK OF FAME

Outside the Chinese Theater in Hollywood, many celebrities have put their hand- and footprints in the concrete. The stars of the Harry Potter movies added imprints of their wands.

A Universal Studio show stuntman re-creates a scene from the movie Waterworld

The footprints, handprints, and wand prints of the Harry Potter stars

A huge simulated set explosion during a live show for visitors to Universal Studios

WOW FACTOR

JAMES CAMERON'S 2009 SCI-FI MOVIE AVATAR SMASHED THE MONEY-MAKING RECORD FOR A HOLLYWOOD BLOCKBUSTER. IT TOOK IN $2,782,275,172 AT THE BOX OFFICE.

Wild about Potter

In 2012 "The Making of Harry Potter" opened at Warner Bros. Studio in Leavesden, near London, England. Fans can see props, costumes, and models and visit the sets of the Great Hall, Dumbledore's office, Diagon Alley, and Hagrid's hut.

MINI HOGWARTS

A hand-painted model of Hogwarts Castle was created for the movies. It measures 50 ft. (15 m) from end to end and contains amazing details such as working doors and miniature owls.

Do you recognize these props?

A scary-looking Slitherin prop on display at the studio.

Web link
For more Potter-tastic details visit
www.wbstudiotour.co.uk

MEET DOBBY

Although many movie special effects are now done on computer, some are "animatronics"—mechanical puppets covered with latex skin. Dobby the house elf is a good example.

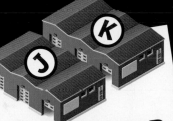

WOW FACTOR

THE TWO HANGARS HOUSING THE TOUR ARE NAMED "J" AND "K." CAN YOU GUESS WHY?

THE AUTHOR OF THE HARRY POTTER BOOKS IS NAMED J. K. ROWLING.

MOVIE MAGIC

Here are some fabulous facts about the magical Harry Potter movies:

- A total of 588 sets were created for the movie series. The biggest set was the Ministry of Magic.
- Harry Potter actor Daniel Radcliffe wore out 60–70 wands and used 160 pairs of glasses during the moviemaking.
- The Australian embassy in London was used as a movie location for Gringotts Bank.

READY, SETS, GO!

In *Harry Potter and the Sorcerer's Stone*, Harry speaks parseltongue for the first time in the Reptile House at London Zoo. A plaque marks the spot now, although it's a black mamba rather than a Burmese python that you'll find inside the nearby display case.

A re-creation of Diagon Alley, where Harry and his friends got their wands.

ALL ABOARD FOR HOGWARTS

If you're passing through London's King's Cross Station, don't forget to visit Platform 9 ¾. A luggage cart that looks as though it is disappearing into the wall has been placed on the train station concourse to mark the secret departure point of the Hogwarts Express train.

CATCH THE KNIGHT BUS

The Knight Bus from *Harry Potter and the Prisoner of Azkaban* was pieced together from three vintage London double-decker buses. Two versions were built—a motorized one that could be driven and a stunt one that could spin around.

New Zealand: One Location to Rule Them All

The landscapes of New Zealand helped director Peter Jackson bring J. R. R. Tolkien's books to our screens in *The Lord of the Rings* and *The Hobbit*. Many "Tolkien tourists" now go to New Zealand, but the locations are far apart. Getting to them all is a quest worthy of Frodo and Bilbo.

HOME FOR HOBBITS

The set for Frodo Baggins's hometown in the Shire was built at Alexander Farm near Matamata. The set was planted with grass and flowers a year before filming to make sure it looked natural. A permanent Hobbiton set has now been built there, and visitors can see the hobbit holes, the mill, and the Green Dragon Inn.

Can you name these Middle Earth movie characters?

THE FORD OF BRUINEN

The scene in *The Fellowship of the Ring* in which Arwen protects Frodo by summoning waves of white horses was filmed on the Shotover Rover near Arrowtown, which sounds a little like a location from one of the original Tolkien books!

WOW FACTOR

TOURISM TO NEW ZEALAND INCREASED BY 50% AFTER THE RELEASE OF THE LORD OF THE RINGS TRILOGY. "TOLKIEN TOURISTS" SWARMED TO THE FILMING LOCATIONS, SOME OF THEM EVEN DRESSED AS CHARACTERS FROM THE MOVIES.

THE MISTY MOUNTAINS

A mountain range with the remarkable name of the Remarkables, overlooking Queenstown on the South Island, stood in for the Misty Mountains in both *The Lord of the Rings* and *The Hobbit*.

FANGORN FOREST

Snowdon Forest on the South Island stood in for Fangorn Forest in *The Two Towers*. It is just as green and dense in real life, though sadly the trees don't talk back.

LOTHLORIEN

The Fernside Lodge estate in Walrarapa, North Island, stood in for Lothlorien, home of elven queen Galadriel. A white bridge was built there for the scene in which Galadriel parts with the Fellowship.

WELCOME, MY PRECIOUS!

You don't even have to leave the airport in New Zealand's capital, Wellington, to spot something from *The Lord of the Rings*. A giant sculpture of Gollum grabbing a fish welcomes visitors.

MOUNT DOOM

Tongariro National Park was the location for Mordor, Frodo's final destination. The site contains three volcanoes, including Mount Ngauruhoe (left), which stood in for Mount Doom. It doesn't have a giant fiery eye on top, but it is active and capable of erupting. It's possible to climb, though the route is steep and dangerous, just like Mount Doom itself.

SUPER
CIRQUE DU SOLEIL

A live show can be a thrilling night out, especially at the world-famous Cirque du Soleil.
Find out about all the fun.

Web link
Find out more about the amazing circus at www.cirquedusoleil.com

OUCH!

SOLEIL STYLE

Cirque du Soleil was founded in Quebec, Canada, in 1984. It has since grown into one of the largest entertainment companies in the world and has helped change our idea of what a circus is. Instead of animals, it features only human performers, such as dancers, acrobats, and clowns, in spectacular shows.

* Cirque du Soleil means "Circus of the Sun."

* More than 100 million people have seen a Cirque du Soleil show since it was founded.

* Performers from all over the world train at the Creation Studio in Montreal, where new shows are planned and put together.

STATS AND FACTS FROM CIRQUE DU SOLEIL

▸ Cirque du Soleil was founded by two French-Canadian street performer friends.

▸ Its logo is a smiling sun.

▸ Its performances have themes and characters, like theater plays, and feature live music.

▸ It has performed at many major events, including the Super Bowl and the Oscars.

The world's most skilled acrobats perform at Cirque du Soleil shows, acting out different themes.

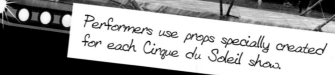

Performers use props specially created for each Cirque du Soleil show.

How does David Copperfield do that?

WORLDWIDE MAGIC

Acrobatic shows such as Cirque du Soleil may be popular, but it's magicians who are the worldwide superstars of live entertainment. American maestro David Copperfield (left) is one of the best known, performing wonders at some of the planet's top locations. He even made the Statue of Liberty "disappear," and he appeared to pass through the Great Wall of China.

BRILLIANT BLUE

The American Blue Man Group have become one of the most unusual worldwide live performing hits. They put music, dance, and mime into their stage shows, but no words. The performers cover their hands and faces completely with blue makeup.

04

> The liveliest, craziest, funniest, silliest, biggest, weirdest, smartest, most exciting, eye-popping, amazing, skilled, most popular . . .

CULTURAL WONDERS

The Harbin Snow and Ice Sculpture Festival, p. 74

RIO CARNIVAL

The world's biggest party takes place every spring in Rio de Janeiro, Brazil, when the Carnival comes to town.

All the costumes are themed, such as this flower outfit.

FOUR-DAY FUN

The Carnival is a megaparty that has been going for hundreds of years. It runs over four noisy fun-filled days before the religious period of Lent, when many Christians traditionally give up rich foods and parties. Around two million people come out onto the streets to see the show and take part. There are parades and street festivals around the city, and the climax of the Carnival is the samba school competition at the Sambadrome.

DANCING TO VICTORY

Around 200 samba schools take part in the contest, but they are not really schools. They are neighborhood social clubs made up of people who together spend months preparing for the celebration. Each school picks a theme and creates costumes, floats, and dances for a performance. Up to 4,000 people might perform in a samba school accompanied by bands playing rhythmic music with a fast beat.

The samba schools build amazing floats based on open-topped trucks.

Samba school members spend all year creating gorgeous costumes for the party.

SAMBA SPORT

Rio's samba schools have their own sports-style league, with different divisions. The top schools compete for the championship in the Sambadrome at Carnival time, watched by judges. Everyone in a school will have a role in the competition performance, with a particular place either on a float or marching along.

WOW FACTOR

SAMBA MUSIC AND DANCING WERE INTRODUCED TO BRAZIL BY WEST AFRICAN PEOPLE WHO WERE ORIGINALLY BROUGHT OVER AS SLAVES.

Samba drums provide the Carnival sound track.

Venice Carnivale

01

02

Holi festival

PARTY ROUND THE WORLD

01. Venice is also famous for its springtime Carnivale, held before Lent. Participants wear mysterious masks to hide their faces.

02. Hindus celebrate the colorful spring festival of Holi by throwing colored flour and water over each other.

03. In Thailand the new year is celebrated in April with Songkran, when everyone takes to the streets with buckets and hoses, soaking each other for fun.

03

Songkran festival

FUN FOR FOOD FANS

Some world parties focus on food, and it can get messy ...

FOOD FIGHT!

The town of Ivrea, Italy, has its own unusual spring carnival just before Lent. The highlight is a giant town food fight called the Battle of the Oranges. Nine teams of locals pelt one another with oranges to commemorate the legend of the townspeople defying a local medieval tyrant, who ended up having his head cut off. The carnival ends with a solemn procession representing the loser's funeral.

Spectators at the Battle of the Oranges are encouraged to wear red caps so that they don't get oranges aimed at them.

WHO'S WHO IN THE ORANGE BATTLE?

The orange-chucking teams (the "Aranceri," or "orange handlers") are split between orange-throwers on foot, representing the townspeople, and orange-chuckers in carts, representing the tyrant's troops.

YUM YUM BUGS

The Hokitika Wild Food Festival in New Zealand has its own unusual take on the food theme. It celebrates and serves up wild food found locally, and its specialty is the huhu grub, the larva of a common New Zealand beetle. At the festival stalls you can chow down on the huhu grub pickled, barbecued, chocolate-coated, or battered. Some snack show-offs even try eating the grubs live.

A WARM WELCOME TO SPRING

Ivrea's crazy carnival and many other springtime festivals go back to very ancient times when people celebrated the end of winter and the coming of spring, sometimes offering sacrifices and thanks to the gods that they thought controlled the seasons. Ivrea's celebrations include a giant bonfire, as do many old festivals with ancient roots.

If you don't fancy the grubs at Hokitika (being munched above), other wild foods are available, such as wasp-larvae ice cream, grasshoppers in Jell-O, and crispy coastal shark.

Chinchilla Melon Festival, Australia:
Celebrate watermelons every February by putting them on your feet and skiing, or enter competitions such as seed spitting.

La Tomatina, Buñol, Spain:
Join 45,000 people throwing squishy tomatoes at one another every August.

Night of the Radishes, Oaxaca City, Mexico: On December 23 carved radishes are displayed, showing nativity scenes and saints.

FUNNY FOOD FESTS

Here are some more tasty food festivals.

Let's go to THAT!

Do you like the idea of a party with a difference? Then step up for one of these truly unusual celebrations.

HOOTING AT HUNGER

The Ga people of Ghana celebrate the Homowo Festival, which translates as "hooting at hunger." In June loud noise is banned so that the growing crops will not be disturbed, but in August there is a noisy party to celebrate the harvest.

WATCH OUT FOR THAT BABY!

Castrillo de Murcia, Spain, hosts a June baby-jumping festival to celebrate a religious feast day. Men dressed as the devil jump over rows of babies lying on mattresses in the street.

MASK-MAKING MOMENT

The Dogon people of Mali are famous for their amazing masks, and in April they hold the Fête des Masques, when the masks are used in ancient rituals to honor the forest spirits that they represent. Every year new masks are carved and placed in a local cave to please the spirits.

GOOD CLEAN FUN

On February 4 the Hadaki Matsuri (Naked Festival) is celebrated in Japan. Participants dressed only in loincloths throw mud and water at one another to symbolize purification.

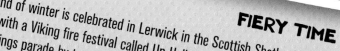

FIERY TIME

The end of winter is celebrated in Lerwick in the Scottish Shetland Islands with a Viking fire festival called Up Helly Aa. Local people dressed as Vikings parade by torchlight and set fire to a Viking-style wooden boat.

MUD-CHUCKING DAY

In July more than a million people come to the Boryeong Mud Festival in South Korea to plaster themselves in mud brought in from a local beach. The mud is said to be good for the skin.

EVERYBODY DANCE!

In April everyone goes dance-crazy in the Punjabi district of India. It is time for Baisakchi, a festival to celebrate the harvest. Everybody has fun dancing bhangra-style in the farm fields.

HOT OR WHAT?

The British village of Ottery St. Mary goes scorchingly crazy on November 5, the night of the Flaming Barrels Festival. Barrels are soaked in tar and their insides are lit. Then, as flames shoot out, locals hoist the barrels on their backs and race through the crowded town. The event may go back to ancient beliefs, but nobody can remember exactly what the evening is about!

HARBIN'S Wonderland

The Harbin Snow and Ice Sculpture Festival is held in northeast China every year in chilly January. It is one of the world's biggest ice sculpture celebrations.

BIG AND BEAUTIFUL

Every evening crowds arrive to walk through "Ice and Snow World," part of the festival where there are many full-size ice buildings lit up with colorful bulbs and sometimes even laser displays. Ice artists from all over the world arrive to help build the frozen art in Harbin and vie to break records for the size of their ice sculptures.

LIGHT IN THE NIGHT

Ice lanterns are an important part of the festival. Traditionally the local fishermen made winter ice lanterns by freezing a block of ice in a bucket and hollowing out the middle to make room for a candle. Nowadays some of the lanterns at the festival are intricately carved works of art.

WOW FACTOR

A RECORD FOR THE TALLEST ICE SCULPTURE WAS SET IN CHINA IN 2010 BY AN ICY DINOSAUR 53 FT. (16.2 M) HIGH.

PERFECTLY COLD

The average winter temperature in Harbin is around –13°F (–25°C), so it's ideal for a frozen festival. Blocks of ice are carved from the local Songhua River to use for the ice sculptures, which are placed all over the city.

SHIVERY SWIM

As well as using the frozen Songhua River for ice blocks, locals like to swim in it! Every winter they carve a swimming pool shape in the frozen surface, and brave swimmers take a dip in the chilly water.

BRRR!

The Holmenkollen Ski Festival:
Norway's March celebration of winter sports, especially ski jumping. Competitors launch themselves from the Homenkollen ski jump (below) and fly up to 463 ft. (141 m) through the air. You can experience the effect yourself in a ski-jump simulator on the site.

The Sapporo Snow Festival:
This Japanese ice fest attracts two million visitors in February. As well as sculptures, it has snow slides and a giant snow maze.

The Quebec City Winter Carnival:
Canada's big February party, with a parade, many snow sculptures, and an ice palace built especially for the carnival mascot, Bonhomme (below).

FROZEN WORLD

Here are some more fabulous world ice festivals.

PITT RIVERS: MUSEUM MADNESS

If you think museums are boring, you're just not looking hard enough! Choose your museum trip carefully and step into a crazy world of weird oddities. We've featured the Pitt Rivers Museum and other surprising spots, but be sure to check out crazy collections near where you live.

REAL WONDERS IN ONE PLACE

The Pitt Rivers Museum in Oxford, England, has more than half a million individual wonders from around the world. It began in 1884 when Lieutenant General Henry Augustus Lane Fox Pitt Rivers donated his collection, and it has since been given all kinds of amazing and unusual objects by explorers and anthropologists (people who study cultures around the globe). The museum (shown right) is kept dark to protect the objects, so it is best for visitors to explore with a flashlight.

HERE ARE JUST A FEW OF THE DISPLAYS TO DISCOVER THERE:

- Inuit clothes made from seal intestines.
- A Pacific island war helmet made from an inflated puffer fish.
- A giant Canadian totem pole.
- Shrunken human heads.
- Hawaiian royal feather cloaks.
- A 120-year-old chunk of cheese.
- A silver bottle said to contain a witch.
- Magical masks.

Web link
Have a look at some of Pitt Rivers's wacky displays: www.prm.ox.ac.uk/

WIG WEIRDNESS

If the Pitt Rivers Museum sounds unusual, try the Avanos Hair Museum in Turkey! More than 16,000 women visitors have donated a strand of hair, and the museum now has the biggest collection of human hair in the world.

The hair is pinned on a cave wall.

HUH?

EVEN WEIRDER..

These museums sound fun!

● The ketchup-red-painted Currywurst Museum in Berlin, Germany, is dedicated to the curried German sausage.

● The International Museum of Toilets in New Delhi, India, is flush with examples of toilets from 2500 BC to today's high-tech versions.

● The Kansas Barbed Wire Museum in LaCrosse, Kansas, has more than 2,000 varieties of what is sometimes called "the devil's rope."

● The Lunchbox Museum in Columbus, Georgia, is the location where lunch boxes are loved the most.

● The British Lawnmower Museum in Southport, England, is a cut above for its collection of the world's greatest grass-trimming equipment.

● The Momofuku Ando Instant Noodle Museum in Osaka, Japan, is a tasty treat for noodle fans. You can invent your own instant noodle flavor there.

WEIRDEST OF ALL?

The Megura Parasitological Museum in Japan specializes in parasites, living things that feed off other living things. Its collection includes a tapeworm measuring 30 ft. (9.1 m), taken from a human, and a dolphin's stomach (shown right) with a lot of worm parasites attached to it.

Terrifically BIG Smithsonian

This museum is the biggest in the world. You'd need years to explore it all, so you'd better start now . . .

THE BIGGEST THERE IS

The Smithsonian Institution is based in the city of Washington, DC. In fact, it is made up of 19 different museums and galleries dotted around the city, all of them free to visitors. If you can't get to Washington, the Smithsonian has its own online Encyclopedia Smithsonian, where you can find out all about its exhibits. On its Web site there are museum-related online games and activities for kids. Check them out using the Web link on the left.

Web link
Find out everything you want to know about the Smithsonian, and spot some cool games and fun activities: www.si.edu

ANIMALS IN THE CITY

The National Zoological Park is part of the Smithsonian. It is home to around 2,000 animals representing almost 400 different species. A fourth of the species are endangered, and the zoo is working to conserve them. Its rare creatures include the Sumatran tiger (left) and western lowland gorillas from Africa.

UP, UP, AND AWAY

The Smithsonian National Air and Space Museum is the world's biggest collection of historic aircraft and spaceships. It has the *Wright Flyer*, the first airplane that ever flew, back in 1903. *The Spirit of St. Louis*, the first airplane ever to fly across the Atlantic nonstop, is also on display, along with hundreds of spacecraft, including a space shuttle (right) in the museum's Udvar-Hazy Center.

DINO NIGHTS

There are many cool natural history museums in the world. Some even let children have sleepovers among the exhibits. For instance, at the Natural History Museum in London, England, you can sleep among dinosaurs!

READY, SETS, GO!

Ben Stiller's sequel movie *Night at the Museum 2* is set in the Smithsonian. The first *Night at the Museum* movie is set in New York's American Museum of Natural History.

TOP TREASURE

The Smithsonian National Museum of Natural History has one of the world's most valuable diamonds, the blue Hope Diamond, set in a necklace (left). Legend has it that the diamond brings bad luck to anyone who wears it.

SISTINE CHAPEL: ART UPSIDE DOWN

One of the world's greatest art treasures is upside down. It is on the ceiling of the Sistine Chapel in Vatican City within Rome, Italy. You have to crane your neck to look up at it, but imagine how the artist felt!

FOUR-YEAR FRESCO

Pope Julius II commissioned the artist Michelangelo to paint the ceiling for him. Michelangelo began the work in 1508 and finished in 1512, taking more than four years to paint the fresco (a painting on plaster). He built a tall wooden scaffold to stand on and had to bend his head backward to paint. His neck must have been very stiff. Afterward he said that the work permanently damaged his eyesight.

PROBLEM PAINTING

Michelangelo had many setbacks as he painted his masterpiece. Mold and damp weather meant that the ceiling plaster would not dry, and his payments were often delayed when the pope went to war or got sick. Michelangelo didn't really want to take on the job at all and continually complained about it.

This painting job was a pain in the neck?

ONLY CLEAN VISITORS ALLOWED

Around five million people visit the Sistine Chapel every year. They bring with them sweat, dust, dandruff, and loose hairs that could damage the ceiling, so a vacuum tunnel has been designed to cut down on the daily dirt. Before sightseers go into the room, they walk through a cleansing tunnel that sucks off dust, cleans the soles of their shoes, and cools them down to stop them from sweating.

BEAUTIFUL FROM BELOW

Michelangelo had to be a master of perspective and color, designing the pictures so that they looked good from 60 ft. (18 m) below on the floor. His pictures show religious scenes such as God's creation of the world. The most famous part of the painting shows God reaching out to touch the finger of Adam, said to be the first man.

A small section of the ceiling fell off after a nearby explosion in 1797.

The ceiling shows more than 300 figures.

Michelangelo considered himself to be a sculptor, not a painter.

In later times an artist was ordered to paint clothing on some of the naked figures on part of the ceiling.

The fresco was painted over the top of a previous fresco that showed the night sky with stars.

Michelangelo had many assistants to help mix plaster and occasionally help with small areas of painting. He often fired them, though.

CHAPEL FACTS

Here are some amazing facts about Michelangelo's upside-down art masterpiece.

OUTDOOR ART

You don't need to go into a gallery or a museum to see amazing art. Just look around you!

WALL WONDERS

Graffiti has become a popular type of outdoor art around the world. The best-known graffiti artists sell their work for a lot of money and get commissioned to decorate the walls of art museums. Some cities designate special areas where graffiti artists can work. In 2012 the city of Bristol, England, made its Nelson Street a graffiti art project, and thousands came to see the walls (shown here).

OOH!

STEP ON IT

Here's some outside art to walk on! The Escardaria Selaron is a flight of 250 stairs in Rio de Janeiro, Brazil, made into a work of art by Chilean artist Jorge Selarón. He covered the stairs with tiles from around the world, creating a popular place for tourists to visit.

PARK PIECES

If you want to see incredible 3-D outside art, explore a sculpture park. The Minneapolis Sculpture Garden in Minnesota is a famous example because of its Spoonbridge and Cherry fountain (above), one of the striking works of Claes Oldenburg and his wife Coosje van Bruggen. They are best known for creating giant models of everyday things.

WOW FACTOR

THE WORLD'S BIGGEST SCULPTURE PARK IS IN CHANGCHUN, CHINA. IT IS FILLED WITH SCULPTURES FROM ALL OVER THE WORLD.

CRAZY GARDENS

Gardens can be interesting outside art, too!

The Step Garden in Fukuoka, Japan, tumbles 196 ft. (60 m) down the side of the Acros building.

The Lost Gardens of Heligan in Cornwall, England, are famous for their plant-covered mud sculptures, including the Giant's Head (above).

The deepest, darkest, murkiest, strangest, most secret, restricted, concealed, isolated, mysterious, surprising, elusive . . .

HIDDEN PLACES

The Cave of Crystals in Mexico, p. 94

AREA 51: NO ENTRY

There are some locations that you're not allowed to visit and, because they're secret, there are all sorts of crazy-sounding theories about them. The most notorious is Area 51, supposedly an alien hot spot. Who knows? Not us!

Is this my 'hood?

ALIEN AREA

Area 51 is a US Air Force base in the Nevada desert. It is strictly out of bounds. Nobody knows why, but there are many far-fetched suggestions. The most famous theory is that an alien spaceship is stored there.

ENTERING AREA 51

TOURIST? TAKE A HIKE!

Visitors aren't welcome within the heavily guarded perimeters of Area 51. Batteries of motion detectors, chemical sensors, and TV cameras are set up to catch any snoopers, and security patrols are authorized to use deadly force on intruders. Don't say we didn't warn you . . .

ALIEN WAY

So many UFO spottings have been reported near Area 51 that the local road has been officially renamed "Extraterrestrial Highway." Do you think all of the mystery flying objects seen here are alien related, or could it be that this base is a test site for secret new Air Force flying technology? It will depend on whether you believe in space visitors or not!

Extraterrestrial Highway NEVADA 375

SPY HEADQUARTERS

Area 51 isn't the only famously out-of-bounds US site. The headquarters of the Central Intelligence Agency (CIA) is in Langley, Virginia, and unsurprisingly you can't wander in. However, you can take a virtual tour on their Web site.

Web link
Take a tour of the CIA! Virtually, of course: https://www.cia.gov/about-cia/headquarters-tour/virtual-tour-flash/index.html

NO-GO DOWN UNDER

Pine Gap is sometimes called Australia's Area 51. It's a top-secret military base southwest of the town of Alice Springs. All kinds of rumors exist about it, including the idea that UFOs visit regularly.

NOT-SO-SECRET SECRETS

One of the oldest secret sites is the Vatican Secret Archives in Vatican City. There thousands of historical documents are stored on more than 50 mi. (80 km) of shelves. However, it's no longer as secret as it once was, and researchers can request to look at documents.

The golfball shapes at Pine Gap are radomes. They contain big dish-shaped antennae that track satellites.

BURLINGTON BUNKER: FOUND UNDERGROUND

The Burlington Bunker was like a whole town hidden underground. Discover its secrets and spy out some other secret subsoil locations.

BOMB BUNKER

During the Cold War of the 1950s–1980s, many nuclear bunkers were built. These were deep shelters meant to protect people from the blasts of nuclear bomb explosions. Nuclear war was avoided, but the bunkers remain, and one of the largest was a hidden underground complex near the town of Corsham, England. It was code-named the Burlington Bunker.

The inside of the Burlington Bunker was kitted out for an underground stay.

THREE MONTHS . . . THEN YOU'D NEED TO GO SHOPPING

The Burlington Bunker had enough room for 4,000 government officials, including the British prime minister. It was more than 0.6mi. (1 km) long, and a fleet of battery-powered carts navigated its 10 mi. (16 km) of tunnels. It was bombproof and could provide enough food and water for three months. It was never needed and was finally decommissioned in 2004.

The Burlington Bunker is closed to visitors, but you can take a virtual tour of it at this Web site.

There were beds for all of the people who would have hidden from the nuclear attack.

Web link
Have a look around:
www.burlingtonbunker.co.uk

Hidden in Burlington:

- Hospital rooms ● A TV studio
- Britain's second-biggest telephone exchange
- Kitchens ● Offices ● Bedrooms
- Supply stores ● 12 giant fuel tanks
- An underground lake for drinking water

END-OF-THE-WORLD ADDRESS

Still worried about the world ending? You could pay $50,000 to reserve your space in the Vivos bunker beneath the Mojave Desert. The underground nuclear-proof complex has rooms with TVs, though there might not be much on . . .

The Vivos bunker, for those who think the world might end.

These days the Cu Chi Tunnels are a tourist attraction.

WOW FACTOR

MANY GOVERNMENTS STILL HAVE TOP-SECRET HIDING PLACES PLANNED FOR IMPORTANT PEOPLE IN THE EVENT OF A NUCLEAR ATTACK.

WAR UNDERGROUND

War actually took place underground in the Cu Chi Tunnels, a network running beneath parts of Vietnam. They were dug by the Viet Cong army in their war against South Vietnam and the United States between 1959 and 1975. The tunnels helped them launch surprise attacks and were booby-trapped with bamboo spikes and trip wires that released boxes of scorpions.

PARIS CATACOMBS: SECRETS UNDER THE CITY

Below the pavements of Paris and other world capitals lurk dark dusty places that many people know nothing about.

The bones are carefully arranged in patterns in the Catacombs.

Thousands of human skulls sit under the streets of the French capital city.

CAPITAL CATACOMBS

More than 186 mi. (300 km) of underground tunnels crisscross the city of Paris. They are called the Catacombs. The tunnels were once used by French Revolutionaries and by the Resistance during World War II. In 1871 a group of "Communards" killed a group of "Monarchists" in one of the chambers during conflict in the city.

There are underground tunnels and chambers lined with human bones.

THE CITY OF BONES

In the 1700s the cemeteries of Paris became so overcrowded that they began to stink and pollute city water, so the cemeteries were dug up and the bones were taken down to old stone mines under the city instead. A section of the Catacombs, the L'Ossuaire Municipal, was then used as a burial place and is now thought to contain the bones of around seven million people.

OSSEMENTS DU CIMETIERE DES INNOCENTS DÉPOSÉS LE 2 JUILLET 1809

A secret presidential railroad track hides under Grand Central Station.

PRESIDENT'S PERK

Paris isn't the only city with a secret. Underneath Grand Central Station in New York City there is an abandoned stretch of railroad known as "Track 61," used by President Franklin D. Roosevelt in the 1930s. He was in a wheelchair, but the government didn't want the public to know, so they used secret elevators to take him from his train via Track 61 into the nearby Waldorf Hotel.

HIDDEN DISNEY

Visitors to Walt Disney World in Florida are actually walking on top of a secret network of tunnels. Wide "utility corridors" run underneath the theme park so that staff in costumes can move around without being seen in the wrong themed area. That's why you won't see someone dressed as a cowboy in the futuristic area or a spaceman in the Wild West area.

STALIN'S SUBWAY

The Russian government has never confirmed the existence of the "Metro 2," a secret subway system beneath Moscow's regular Metro. Many claim that the secret network links sites such as airports, army bases, and nuclear bunkers. It was supposedly built in the time of Russian leader Joseph Stalin (above) and connected to his house.

UNDERGROUND ARTISTS

It is dangerous to visit the Paris tunnels without a guide, but Parisians with inside knowledge, nicknamed "cataphiles," like to explore the tunnels in secret, risking capture by a special Catacomb police patrol. Some have painted pictures, made sculptures, and performed plays down there. A secret cinema was even created once, with seats carved in the stone.

FORT KNOX LOCKED AWAY

Some things are so valuable that they need to be hidden where no thief will ever get to them. That's why there are impenetrable bank vaults such as Fort Knox.

GOVERNMENT GOLD

The United States Bullion Depository at Fort Knox in Kentucky (shown below) is thought to hold thousands of gold bars on behalf of the US government. Around 3% of all the gold ever processed is inside Fort Knox.

NOT JUST GOLD

During World War II, Fort Knox provided safe shelter for important documents such as the US Declaration of Independence and the UK Magna Carta. It also kept the Hungarian crown safe.

The Magna Carta at Fort Knox.

READY, SETS, GO!

In the James Bond movie *Goldfinger*, the villain's plan is to set off a nuclear bomb inside Fort Knox, making the gold radioactive and driving up the price of his own supply.

DON'T EVEN THINK ABOUT IT

Nobody has ever tried to steal the gold from Fort Knox. Its vault has granite walls, blast-proof doors, and state-of-the-art security. The building is surrounded by armed soldiers and an army base with helicopter gunships and tanks. No visitors are ever allowed in the building.

UNITED STATES DEPOSITORY

WHO HAS THE GOLD?

Which countries have the most gold locked away in their vaults? Here are the top five national gold reserves thought to be in storage.

1. United States–8,965 tons (8,133.5 tonnes)
2. Germany–3,738 tons (3,391.3 tonnes)
3. Italy–2,702 tons (2,451.8 tonnes)
4. France–2,684 tons (2,435.4 tonnes)
5. China–1,161 tons (1,054.1 tonnes)

THE BIG ONE

The biggest gold stash in the world is in the New York Federal Reserve Vault, 79 ft. (24 m) below Liberty Street in New York City. Visitors can take a guided tour but no glittery souvenirs.

WOW FACTOR

THE GOLD BARS IN THE BANK OF ENGLAND ARE REGULARLY DUSTED BY A CLEANER.

THE KEY

Underneath the Bank of England, on London's Threadneedle Street, there's a vault storing piles of gold bars. They belong to the United Kingdom and several other countries that don't have a safe place to keep their stash. The doors are so thick that the key to open them is 3 ft. (91 cm) long.

GOLD STASH STATS

THESE FIGURES ARE APPROXIMATE. NOBODY IS ADMITTING TO THE TRUE SIZE OF THE STORES!

NEW YORK FEDERAL RESERVE–7,716 TONS (7,000 TONNES)

BANK OF ENGLAND–5,070 TONS (4,600 TONNES)

FORT KNOX–5,046.3 TONS (4,578 TONNES)

AMAZING CAVES

LOOK INSIDE!

Tourists all over the world are drawn to the amazing rock formations found inside caves. Here are some spectacular sights worth venturing underground for.

ANCESTOR ART

Ancient humans have left art on cave walls around the world, showing the animals that they hunted and their own handprints. The Cave of Altamira in Spain is one of the best examples, but human breath damages cave paintings, so only a few people can visit at a time.

CRYSTAL CAVE

The Cave of Crystals, near Chihuahua, Mexico, is filled with giant crystals up to 36 ft. (11 m) long. Explorers must wear breathing apparatus and special suits filled with ice cubes to keep themselves from overheating in the hot, humid, and deadly atmosphere of the cave.

A ROOM WITH A VIEW

You can take a boat trip down the Puerto Princesa underground river in the Philippines to see the Italian's Chamber, one of the largest cave halls in the world. At 1,181 ft. (360 m) long and 262 ft. (80 m) high, it is as big as a cathedral.

WOW FACTOR

WITHOUT BREATHING EQUIPMENT, HUMANS COULD SURVIVE FOR ONLY TEN MINUTES INSIDE THE CAVE OF CRYSTALS.

HANGING DOWN

Stalactites hang down like icicles from the roofs of limestone caves. One of the world's biggest stalactites is in the Jeita Grotto caves in Lebanon. It hangs 27 ft. (8.2 m) down from the roof.

DARE YOU JUMP?

Thrill seekers from all over the world are drawn to the Cave of the Swallows in Mexico. It's the largest known cave shaft in the world, and daring BASE jumpers have been known to jump into the 1,093 ft. (333 m) drop.

Stalagmite

EEK!

Stalactite

WONDROUS WORMS

In the Waitomo Glowworm Caves, on New Zealand's North Island, the walls are covered in thousands of tiny glowworms. They radiate a green-yellow color, creating one of the world's most unusual light shows.

GOING UP

Stalagmites form on the grounds of caves, sticking up like traffic cones. The world's largest stalagmite is in the Cueva Martin Infierno in Cuba. It rises 197 ft. (60 m) up from the floor.

Web link

Find a cave to visit near you: www.showcaves.com/english/usa/index.html

BARROW & CO.

Feel like getting away from it all? Here are some of the world's most isolated settlements, starting with a chilly northern city where the ground is permanently frozen.

A COOL PLACE TO LIVE

Barrow, Alaska, is the northernmost city in the United States. It is 320 mi. (515 km) north of the Arctic Circle on the tundra, where the ground is permanently frozen and no trees grow. It stays dark for two whole months there in the winter, but despite the town's extreme conditions, it's home to more than 4,000 people.

WOW FACTOR

THE LOCAL INUPIAT PEOPLE FIRST CALLED BARROW "UKPEAGUIK," MEANING "WHERE SNOW OWLS ARE HUNTED."

KEEP YOUR COAT ON

Barrow has a polar climate, which means that it is very cold and dry. In fact, it is classified as a desert because it has so little rainfall. The temperature stays below freezing from October to May, so everybody has to wrap up warm. It is also one of the cloudiest places on the planet.

TOUGH TRAVELING:

Here are some other tough-to-reach locations that need careful travel plans:

- Ittoqqortoormiit is on the Greenland coast, where the ocean is frozen for most of the year. The only way to reach it is by helicopter. Around 500 people live there.

- Tristan da Cunha, in the South Atlantic, is the world's most isolated inhabited island. Around 300 people live there, and the only way to get there is by boat. The nearest neighboring community is 1,350 mi. (2,173 km) away.

- La Rinconada, Peru, is the highest city in the world. It is 16,732 ft. (5,100 m) above sea level and can only be reached by truck.

- The town of Supai is at the bottom of the Grand Canyon in Arizona. There are no roads, and a 9 mi. (14.4 km) hike is needed to get there. The mail is delivered by mule.

- Motuo County in China can be reached only by walking through the Himalayas and crossing a suspension bridge. All attempts to build a road have been thwarted by mudslides and avalanches.

THE PARTY'S JUMPING

Barrow was founded by the local Inupiat people, and hunting animals for meat and skins is their way of life. In June the end of a successful whale-hunting season is celebrated with a special Inupiat party and ceremony—the Natukataq Blanket Toss. A giant trampoline is made from sealskins and everybody has a go at jumping as high as they can.

NOW THAT'S COLD!

The village of Oymyakon in the Sakha Republic, Russia, beats Barrow for coldness. It has the record for the lowest temperature in any permanently inhabited location. It has been known to reach a bone-chilling –90°F (–67.7°C) there.

La Rinconada, Peru, lays claim to being the highest city in the world.

SUTTON HOO: LOST AND FOUND

Sometimes objects that seemed lost can turn up in very surprising places, but imagine finding a tomb full of treasure or a lost palace!

MYSTERY MAN

In 1939 archaeologists digging at Sutton Hoo in England discovered the remains of a man who had been buried in a ship more than 1,300 years earlier. Many precious objects were buried with the body, including coins, jewelry, weapons, and an iron helmet decorated with scenes of battles and animals. Nobody knows for sure who was buried there, but it's thought that it may be Redwald, a powerful local ruler in the 600s.

YOU COME, TOO

Several ship burials have been found in northern Europe, and other people seem to have been sacrificed alongside the main burial. Perhaps servants were chosen to go with the dead person to the afterlife.

Web link
Find similar discoveries in the British Museum's online tours: www.britishmuseum.org/explore/online_tours.aspx

The front of the iron-and-bronze Sutton Hoo helmet is decorated with a dragon-bird. Its wings make eyebrows, and its tail creates a mustache.

LOADED BOAT

The Sutton Hoo king was buried in his boat to go on a journey to the afterlife, along with the treasures he needed. There was a purseful of gold coins to pay the ghostly oarsmen who his followers thought would row him to a heavenly kingdom, where he could feast using his cooking cauldron and drinking horn. Over time the wood of the king's boat rotted away, but its shape was still found imprinted in the ground.

The shape of the Sutton Hoo boat was imprinted in the ground where it had been buried.

WOW FACTOR

PALACE OF THE MINOTAUR

If finding a ship sounds exciting, how about a whole palace? At the end of the 1800s archaeologists unearthed a huge palace at Knossos on the island of Crete. Inside they found paintings, objects, and written records from the ancient civilization of the Minoans. The palace was made famous in Greek myth for being the legendary home of a giant half-man and half-bull beast called the Minotaur.

Tourists can visit the excavated palace at Knossos, mythical home of the Minotaur.

GOLDEN FIND

One of the most glittering treasure finds of all came to light in Egypt's Valley of the Kings in 1922, when Howard Carter uncovered the tomb of Tutankhamen, a pharaoh from the 14th century BC. The tomb contained fabulous treasures, such as the king's golden burial mask. As if all this wasn't exciting enough, the newspapers invented a story about Carter being cursed by Tutankhamen for breaking into his tomb.

Howard Carter's team exploring Tutankhamen's tomb.

STILL MISSING

During World War II, one of Russia's greatest art treasures, the Amber Room, was taken from a Russian palace by German troops. The treasures and amber panels that made up the fabulous room were lost, and though many have searched, nobody has yet rediscovered them.

A modern reconstruction of the Amber Room.

TERRACOTTA ARMY

Farmers digging a well in Xi'an, China, in 1974 came across some spectacular life-size clay sculptures. They turned out to be part of the "Terracotta Army" of Qin Shi Huang, the first emperor of China.

MODEL SOLDIERS

The site contains more than 8,000 life-size soldiers, all with individual clothing, hair, and facial features. They are arranged in pits around the emperor's burial complex, as if to guard him in the afterlife. In addition to the warriors, there are clay sculptures of entertainers and officials and excellently preserved bronze weapons.

Archaeologists are still busy uncovering the vast site in Xi'an.

THE MERCURY MAN

Emperor Qin Shi Huang lived from 259 BC to 210 BC. He was obsessed with immortality and spent years seeking the elixir of life, a mythical potion that would let him live forever. In fact, some experts think that he may have been killed, at age 39, by mercury pills that he thought would make him immortal. Far from providing eternal life, mercury is deadly poisonous.

STILL HIDDEN

The emperor's actual tomb has been located, but it hasn't yet been opened. Ancient writers said that Qin Shi Huang had the tomb built as an entire underground palace, surrounded by rivers of silver mercury. Tests in the soil around the tomb show very high levels of mercury, so excavating is going to be difficult and dangerous. Scientists are waiting until they're sure that they have the right technology to look inside without damaging the contents.

IN THE PITS

Here are some of the treasures found in Xi'an:

Human figures to entertain the emperor, such as acrobats, dancers, and singers.

Clay government officials to help the Emperor rule his kingdom in the afterlife.

Different types of soldiers, including cavalry, archers, foot soldiers, and charioteers.

Life-size sculptures of horses with wooden chariots (one shown above).

The coolest, cleverest, most surprising, expensive, amazing, unbelievable, advanced, fastest, toughest, coldest, cleanest, and most polluted science spots in the world. It's time for . . .

HIGH TECH

The Paranal Observatory in Chile, p. 117

AUTOSTADT: Wheely GOOD

Bet you never thought parking lots could be amazing! Check out these fabulous parking spots, starting with some cool automated towers.

TOWERS OF POWER

A car theme park called Autostadt stands next to the Volkswagen factory in Wolfsburg, Germany. There is a car museum, driving tracks, restaurants, and stores, but Autostadt is most famous for its automated car towers. There are two of them, both 200 ft. (60 m) tall and housing 400 cars each. If you buy a new VW, you can come here and watch your car robotically arrive from one of the towers.

HERE COMES THE CAR

An underground tunnel brings cars from the factory to the towers, and they are carried up to parking bays on giant automatic platforms (above). When a car is needed, a platform zooms up, the car comes out of its bay, and the platform zooms back down. Visitors can take a guided ride around the towers to watch the automated fun.

CAR ART

Unlike the Autostadt, the cars at Carhenge in Alliance, Nebraska, are parked forever! This re-creation of the famous Stonehenge monument in England uses 38 gray-painted cars instead of standing stones. Artist Jim Reinders built it as a tribute to his dad, and now the area around is known as the Car Art Reserve, with other recycled car sculptures to see.

Travelers voted Carhenge the second-wackiest tourist site in the US, after the Toilet Seat Art Museum in San Antonio.

WOW FACTOR

THE LARGEST COMPUTERIZED "SMART" PARKING LOT IS IN DUBAI, WITH ROOM FOR AROUND 1,200 CARS. THE CARS ARE LEFT BY THEIR DRIVERS TO BE MOVED AROUND AUTOMATICALLY ON ELEVATORS.

www.autostadt.de

I LOVE MY MOTOR

Architect Takuya Tsuchida designed the KRE house in Tokyo for a car-nut with a beloved vehicle collection. The house has room for nine cars in the garage and a car elevator to bring one up to the living room, to look at admiringly or to show off to guests.

BONNEVILLE AND BEYOND

Welcome to the world's top spots for speedsters, the go-to locations where driving speed records are regularly smashed.

SHOOTING THE SALT

Bonneville Salt Flats in Utah is one of the best superspeed tracks on the planet. Its slick salt surface is all that remains of an ancient lake, providing a lot of space for record drives. The first land speed record was set there in 1914, and since then it has hosted many record attempts, sometimes described as "shooting the salt." All kinds of vehicles have set records there, including cars, motorcycles, (left) and streamliners–aerodynamic vehicles that can reach speeds of more than 500 mph (800 kph).

WOW FACTOR

TO HAVE A SPEED RECORD CONFIRMED, A VEHICLE HAS TO MAKE TWO RUNS ALONG A COURSE WITHIN ONE HOUR.

The JCB DieselMax (below) set the fastest diesel car record at Bonneville in 2006, reaching 350 mph (563 kph).

JCB DIESELMAX

CHOOSING WISELY

Anyone attempting to break a driving speed record must choose a flat location where the weather is warm and dry and there is a lot of room to speed up and slow down. The course must be stone free, so before record attempts stone pickers walk the course and carefully remove anything that might look dangerous. If the front wheel of a superspeeding car flicked up a stone, it could smack into the car at the speed of a bullet. That's why cars attempting land speed records have bulletproof wheels.

Web link
Follow the next attempt at the world land speed record:
www.bloodhoundssc.com/

Goldenrod, a famous piston-driven car record holder at Bonneville in 1965. It reached 409 mph (658 kph).

READY, SETS, GO!

Desolate-looking Bonneville Flats appears in many movies and TV shows, including *Independence Day* and *Pirates of the Caribbean: At World's End.*

BLACK ROCK ON TOP

The Black Rock Desert rivals Bonneville as the best speed spot. It is a vast dry lava bed in the Nevada wilderness, and it was there in 1997 that ThrustSSC (right) became the first supersonic vehicle ever. Driven by British ex-pilot Andy Green, it went faster than the speed of sound to set a new land speed record of 760.343 mph (1,223.657 kph). The car was powered by two turbojets from a fighter jet airplane.

COMING SOON IN SOUTH AFRICA

Land speed record holder Andy Green is planning to increase the record using a streamlined car called Bloodhound, with the power of 180 Formula One cars (a scale model is shown left). The record will be attempted on Hakskeen Pan in South Africa, which suits the car better than Black Rock or Bonneville. The Bloodhound team used the mapping technology of Google Earth to come up with the site, which had to be flat, firm, and at least 9 mi. (16 km) long, with plenty of room at each end.

www.jcbdieselmax.com

RICARDO corus UGS 440AA/DS

SPACE BASES

Where is the best place to see rockets blasting off into space? Check out these spaceports, where the out-of-this-world action happens.

First Moon Landing, 1969

I went by rocket!

THEY MADE IT TO THE MOON

The Kennedy Space Center near Orlando, Florida, was responsible for the launch of all of the United States' Apollo manned space-flight missions. Its experts were in control as Apollo 11 became the first spaceship to land humans on the Moon, in 1969, and they guided astronauts Neil Armstrong and Buzz Aldrin on their historic first Moon walks.

SPACE VISITORS WELCOME

As well as being a functioning launch site, the Kennedy Space Center offers visitors a tour through the history of the United States' space program. In the Rocket Garden (right) you can see the huge Atlas and Titan rockets that blasted the astronauts in their Apollo modules off into space. You can even climb into one of the modules to see how cramped the conditions were.

Web link
NASA has its own live TV station:
www.nasa.gov/multimedia/nasatv/index.html

WOW FACTOR

AT THE KENNEDY SPACE CENTER YOU CAN MAKE RESERVATIONS TO HAVE LUNCH WITH A REAL-LIFE ASTRONAUT, WHO WILL TELL YOU ABOUT THEIR WORK.

GO EAST

The world's first space base was the Baikonur Cosmodrome, home of Russia's space program. Situated out in the Kazakhstan desert, this was where Yuri Gagarin became the first man to be launched into space in 1961. It is still operational, sending supply flights to the International Space Station (see p. 110). Its museum has Yuri Gagarin's uniform and a sample of soil from his first landing site, preserved in a silver container.

CCCP

The first woman in space, Valentina Tereshkova, made her space trip from Baikonur in 1963.

UNITED STATES

Baikonur is a busy working spaceport that sends supplies up to the International Space Station.

Virgin Galactic will put tourists in space.

Virgin

LET'S ALL GO!

Soon private citizens will be able to take space journeys around Earth, flying in space planes out beyond the atmosphere. Hundreds of these "space tourists" have already paid deposits to travel in a Virgin Galactic space plane (above), on a trip set to cost around $200,000 per person.

INTERNATIONAL SPACE STATION:
BEDS IN ORBIT

The International Space Station (ISS for short) is a giant space laboratory floating in a low orbit around Earth. Its astronauts live and work there for several months at a time.

TAKE A LOOK AROUND

The station is built from separate parts called modules, which were flown up by spaceship and joined together by spacewalking astronauts. The Zvezda Service Module (shown below) has living accommodation for six crew members.

Work station

Treadmill

Window

SPACE RECYCLING

The water on board the ISS is recycled. Crew members use rinseless shampoo and edible toothpaste to save water, and all of their urine is recycled. Their solid waste is collected, stored, and taken back to Earth.

STRAPPED IN SPACE

Because the ISS is plunging in free fall around Earth, everything on board is weightless and floats. The crew must strap themselves into bed or onto the toilet. They can sleep upright because there is no "up" or "down" on the station.

SPACE GARDEN

ISS astronauts have managed to grow plants from seeds inside boxes called growth chambers. Space crews may be able to grow some of their own fresh food in the future.

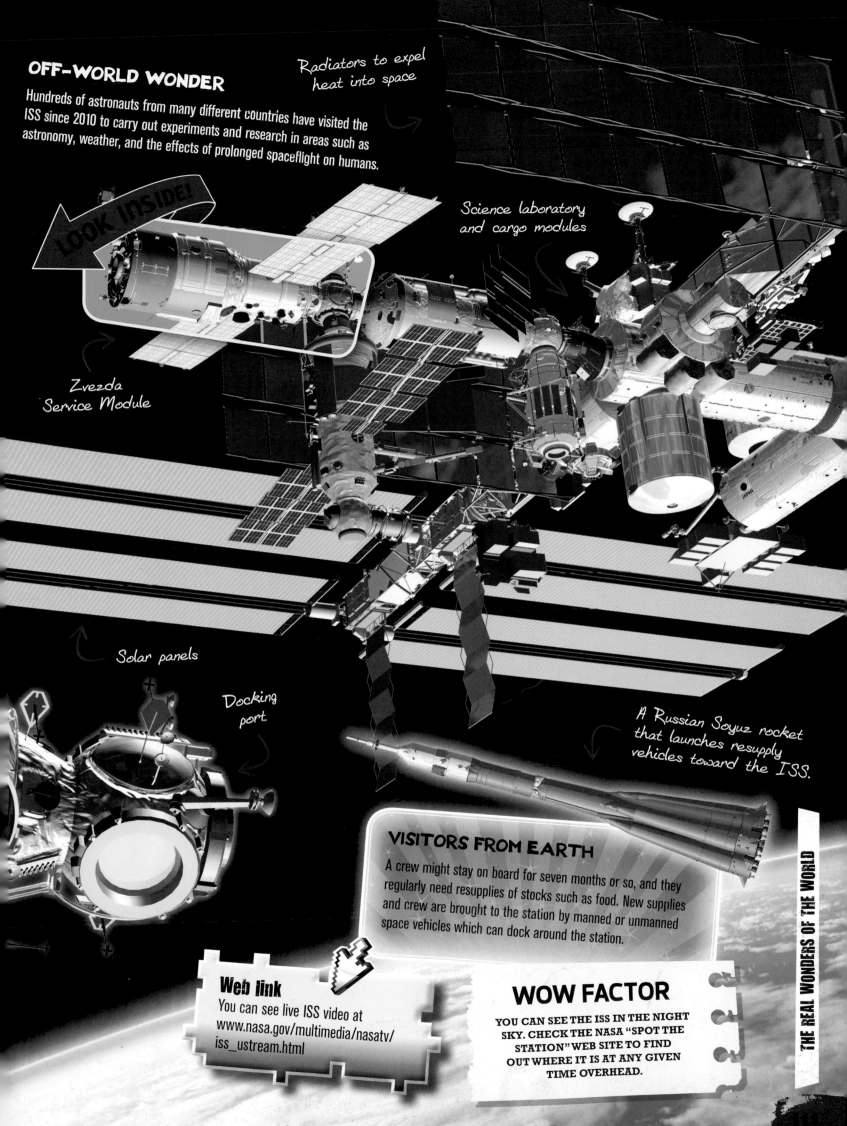

OFF-WORLD WONDER

Hundreds of astronauts from many different countries have visited the ISS since 2010 to carry out experiments and research in areas such as astronomy, weather, and the effects of prolonged spaceflight on humans.

Radiators to expel heat into space

LOOK INSIDE!

Science laboratory and cargo modules

Zvezda Service Module

Solar panels

Docking port

A Russian Soyuz rocket that launches resupply vehicles toward the ISS.

VISITORS FROM EARTH

A crew might stay on board for seven months or so, and they regularly need resupplies of stocks such as food. New supplies and crew are brought to the station by manned or unmanned space vehicles which can dock around the station.

Web link
You can see live ISS video at www.nasa.gov/multimedia/nasatv/iss_ustream.html

WOW FACTOR

YOU CAN SEE THE ISS IN THE NIGHT SKY. CHECK THE NASA "SPOT THE STATION" WEB SITE TO FIND OUT WHERE IT IS AT ANY GIVEN TIME OVERHEAD.

EDEN PROJECT: PLANT POWER

Here are some awesome places where the planet's plants thrive.

BIG BIO-DOMES

The Eden Project is a visitor attraction and not-for-profit organization in Cornwall, England, built in an old quarry. Its giant domes (right) house thousands of plants from around the world for conservation and study. Each dome is made of plastic cells inflated like balloons around steel frames. If they need to be repaired or cleaned, rappellers go up to take care of them. The biggest dome is 180 ft. (55 m) high and 328 ft. (100 m) wide and is tropically warm inside, for growing heat-loving plants such as bananas and coffee.

KEEPING SEEDS SAFE

What would happen if human-made or natural disasters threatened to kill off plants? The answer lies in seed banks, safe storage locations where the world's seeds are kept. The largest seed bank on the planet is the Millennium Seed Bank Partnership housed at Wakehurst Place in England. It has been designed to last for 500 years, and the concrete covering of its flood-proof vaults is thick enough to keep out radiation from nuclear fallout.

CHILLY SEED STORAGE

One of the most important world seed banks is the Svalbard Seed Vault (right) on the Arctic island of Spitsbergen in Norway. It can keep up to 4.5 million seeds safely stored in its underground chambers, hollowed from deep inside a frozen mountain and protected by high-tech security systems.

WHY SO COLD?

Seeds store best when they are cold. At Svalbard the seeds are sealed into moisture-free packets and stored at −0.4°F (−18°C). The site was chosen because it was cold but also because there are no earthquakes or volcanoes there, and at 426 ft. (130 m) above sea level it will remain dry even if the polar ice caps melt through global warming.

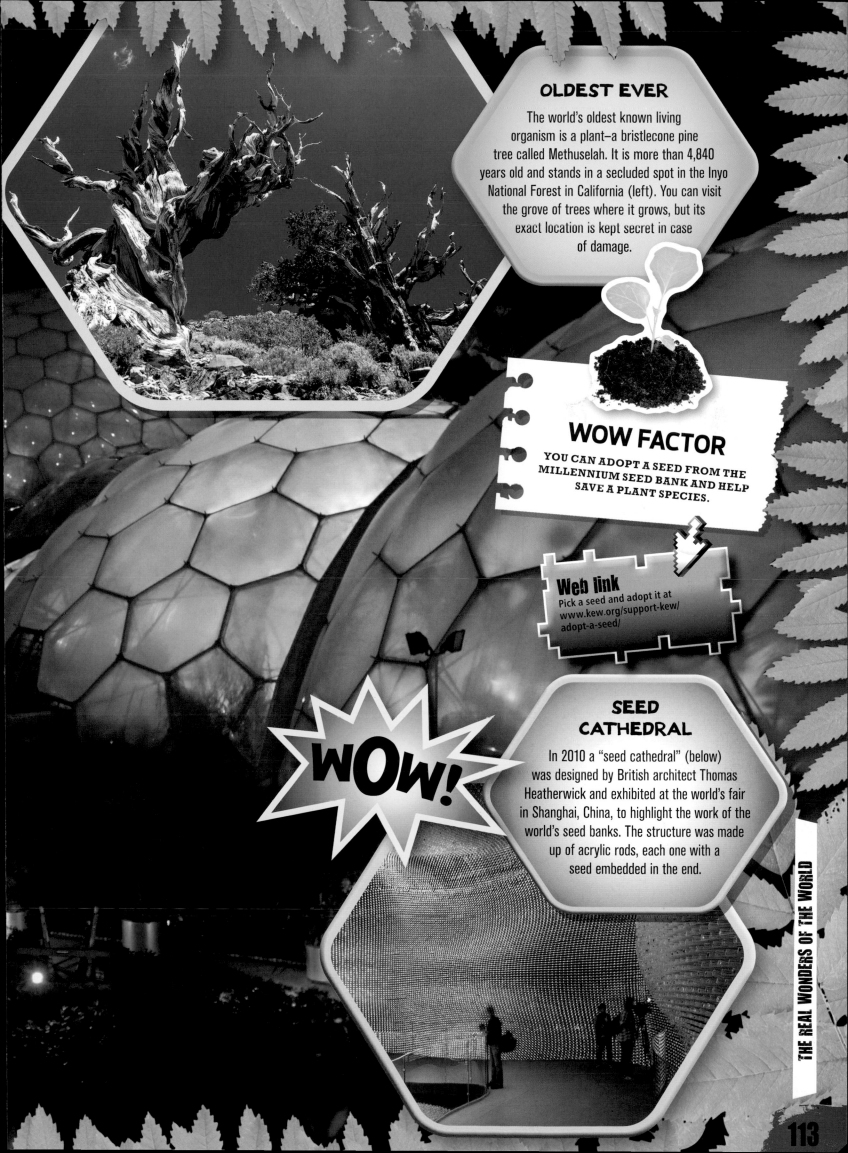

OLDEST EVER

The world's oldest known living organism is a plant—a bristlecone pine tree called Methuselah. It is more than 4,840 years old and stands in a secluded spot in the Inyo National Forest in California (left). You can visit the grove of trees where it grows, but its exact location is kept secret in case of damage.

WOW FACTOR

YOU CAN ADOPT A SEED FROM THE MILLENNIUM SEED BANK AND HELP SAVE A PLANT SPECIES.

Web link
Pick a seed and adopt it at www.kew.org/support-kew/adopt-a-seed/

SEED CATHEDRAL

In 2010 a "seed cathedral" (below) was designed by British architect Thomas Heatherwick and exhibited at the world's fair in Shanghai, China, to highlight the work of the world's seed banks. The structure was made up of acrylic rods, each one with a seed embedded in the end.

WOW!

McMURDO:
WORLD'S ICIEST WORKPLACE

Antarctica is the coldest spot on Earth, and for months of the year it is in total darkness. That makes the US McMurdo Research Station in Antarctica one of the coldest places on the planet for any scientist to work.

McMurdo is built on Ross Island, 2,500 mi. (4,023 km) from New Zealand.

CHILLY CITY

Antarctica does not belong to any one country. Instead it is designated a "continent for science." There are no settlements in Antarctica, only scientific bases. US research station McMurdo is the biggest, so it is sometimes called Antarctica's city. Scientists usually arrive in McMurdo and then travel to other bases around the continent. In the summer around 1,000 people live there, but in the winter only around 200 people stay.

WHY SO TOUGH?

Antarctica is in the far south of the world, and it has six months of continuous daylight in the summer (from September to March), though the average temperature never rises above freezing. In the winter there are six months of continuous darkness, and the temperature can drop to –58°F (–50°C). Inland it can plunge to –100°F (–73°C), and fearsome winds of up to 100 mph (160 kph) whip across the ice.

–58°F

WINTER CHILL

McMurdo can experience winter temperatures nearly three times as cold as a home freezer.

McMurdo workers endure cold weather even in the summer months.

The beautiful aurora australis in the night sky over Antarctica.

- NASA tested its Viking Mars lander in Antarctica because conditions were very cold and dry, rather like Mars.
- In the summer tourists can take Antarctic cruises and sometimes visit research stations.
- The coldest temperature ever recorded on Earth was measured at the Russian Antarctic Vostock Station. It was −128.6°F (−89.2°C).
- The Antarctic ice cap holds 90% of the ice on the planet.
- Penguins visit Antarctica but don't stay year-round. The largest land animal that stays is a wingless midge insect.

FESTIVAL IN THE FRIDGE

As well as bedrooms and science laboratories, McMurdo has a cafeteria, a gym, bars, a bowling alley, a church, a fire station, a post office, and a hospital. In the summer it even holds its own music festival, Icestock (above), when everyone joins in performing and dancing. In the winter, although conditions are tough, the scientists get a fantastic view of the aurora australis, the southern lights, which flicker across the sky.

AS SOUTH AS IT GETS

From McMurdo, scientists travel to the US Amundsen-Scott research station at the South Pole, the southernmost point on Earth. Around fifty people brave the winter months there. Temperatures plunge in the winter and gale-force blizzards can strike, so the base has a rounded shape to help snow slide off.

STARRY SCIENCE

Because Antarctica is in complete darkness for months, and because the air is so clear and cold, it is an ideal place for researching astronomy and Earth's atmosphere. Scientists also drill down into the ice to study it. Divers from McMurdo go under the ice through ice holes drilled into the surface (shown right). They send remote-operated camera vehicles down through the holes, too.

WOW FACTOR

FORTY-TWO SCIENTIFIC BASES BELONGING TO VARIOUS DIFFERENT COUNTRIES ARE MANNED IN ANTARCTICA THROUGH THE WINTER.

atacama STARGAZERS

Is it possible to stand on Earth and see events that occurred almost at the dawn of the universe? Yes, if you go to the Atacama Desert in Chile, where the ALMA telescope gazes out to distant corners of space.

GREAT SPACE VIEW

The ALMA telescope is on a plateau 17,000 ft. (5,000 m) high up in the Chilean desert. Here there is no light pollution (when electric lights brighten the sky and dim the view of space). The dry, clear air helps the radio telescopes work effectively.

SIXTY-SIX DISHES

ALMA has 66 antenna dishes (below), the largest of which are 39 ft. (12 m) wide. The dishes are moved around by giant robotic transporter vehicles, and they can be set up to 10 mi. (16 km) apart in order to point at different areas of space. ALMA cost around $1.4 billion to build, paid for by a number of different countries joining forces.

ALMA DOES ITS STUFF

Telescopes such as ALMA look at ancient galaxies far away in deep space. Astronomers previously found it difficult to see these galaxies because they were shrouded in space dust, but ALMA solves the problem. Even though it opened officially in 2013, it had already gathered images of galaxies that formed 12 billion years ago, one billion years after the birth of the universe.

Web link
See live pictures from ALMA at
www.almaobservatory.org

AMAZING MIRRORS

Chile is such a good stargazing spot that it is also home to the Paranal Observatory (above), which houses the Very Large Telescope (VLT for short). It has four of the largest parabolic (curved) mirrors ever created and has been able to see far into space.

The Horsehead Nebula, an image taken by the VLT at Paranal. A nebula is a giant cloud of dust and gas where stars are born.

A.L.M.A.

WOW FACTOR

ALMA IS SHORT FOR ATACAMA LARGE MILLIMETER/SUB-MILLIMETER ARRAY.

BEST STARGAZING ON THE PLANET

The International Dark Sky Association gives awards to locations for being the best spots in the world to stargaze. Here are some of the places awarded the status of International Dark Sky Parks:

▶ Natural Bridges National Monument, Utah.

▶ Cherry Springs State Park, Pennsylvania.

▶ Galloway Forest Park, Scotland.

▶ Zselic National Landscape Protection Area, Hungary.

Web link

See photos from the world's best stargazing spots at www.darksky.org

SHARP EYES

ALMA detects different types of radiation coming from deep space, created by events such as galaxies forming or stars exploding. It is capable of collecting images that are ten times sharper than those collected by the Hubble Space Telescope in orbit around Earth.

CERN: SMASHING SCIENCE

For cutting-edge science it's hard to beat CERN in Switzerland, a giant science complex where scientists search for mysterious invisible particles that might unlock what happened at the moment the universe was made.

Part of the Large Hadron Collider

ME+3/2/23

INSIDE CERN

Thousands of scientists and engineers from all over the world work at CERN, where the world's largest scientific equipment is being used to study particles—the tiny building blocks that make up everything in the universe. Since work at CERN began, several important particle discoveries have been made, including the discovery of a new type of particle called the Higgs boson.

PARTICLE CRASHING

CERN has a number of particle accelerators—equipment that boosts the speed of particles as they zoom in beams through the machinery. The particles are made to travel as fast as possible, close to the speed of light (the fastest known speed in the universe). Then the particles are made to smash into a stationary object or collide together, an incredibly difficult feat to achieve. Detector equipment gathers all sorts of data from the smash, and physicists use this data to analyze what happened during the collision.

About 186 mi. (300 km) of wires carry information from the LHC.

WOW FACTOR

THE WORLD WIDE WEB—KNOWN AS THE INTERNET—WAS FIRST CREATED AT CERN BY TIM BERNERS-LEE AND ROBERT CAILLIAU. THE FIRST WEB PAGE WAS PUBLISHED FROM CERN IN 1993.

How CERN looks above ground

HUNTING PARTICLES

Everything in existence is made of small parts called molecules. The molecules are made of smaller parts called atoms. The atoms are made of smaller parts called particles, which include protons, neutrons, electrons, and quarks. At CERN, physicists study all of these and look for new ones. They try to figure out what happened when particles were created, at the moment when the universe was born.

Web link
Try CERN games and puzzles at www.cernland.net

LHC COLLIDER FACTS

▶ Each particle beam consists of around 3,000 particle bunches, each containing 100 billion proton particles.

▶ At close to light speed, the protons in the LHC make around 11, 245 laps of the tunnel each second.

▶ The central part of the LHC is equivalent to the world's largest freezer. It is kept even colder than the temperature out in deep space.

▶ Staff at CERN use bicycles to move around the giant tunnel.

LHC—THE BIG SMASHER

CERN's biggest particle accelerator is its Large Hadron Collider (LHC for short). This giant underground circular tunnel is 328 ft. (100 m) below the ground and measures 16 mi. (27 km) around. Beams of proton particles are injected at top speed into the Large Hadron Collider, where they whiz around in a vacuum (airless atmosphere) and collide. Giant magnets keep the proton beams in position.

LINFEN: TRASH CITY

The world's most polluted city is currently said to be Linfen, China. Find out about this smoggy spot and other polluted places.

TOXIC TOWN

In Linfen the coal industry produces choking dust-filled air and stinking toxic gases such as carbon dioxide and sulfur dioxide, which are harmful to the three million people who live there.

In 2007 Linfen residents suffered 163 days of heavily polluted air. Since then it has gradually improved.

STREETS OF DISEASE

Levels of pollution in Linfen are many times higher than the safe limit set by the World Health Organization. This causes diseases such as bronchitis, pneumonia, and lung cancer. The children of Linfen have very high levels of lead poisoning.

FACTORY FOG

Linfen's industry has developed very quickly, and there are many mines, factories, and refineries. They use up so much water that it has to be rationed. But now Linfen is trying to clean up, and much cleaner, more high-tech industrial complexes are replacing the polluting ones.

This photo shows smog (polluted air) shrouding Linfen like a murky yellow fog.

Jardim Gramacho in Brazil was the world's biggest garbage dump until it closed in 2012. Waste pickers lived on the dump, sifting through the trash and selling it on.

The Great Pacific Garbage Patch is a giant area of the North Pacific where tiny slivers of plastic from dumped garbage have gathered beneath the water. They whirl around in a giant circle said to be bigger than the United States. No sea life can survive there.

Guiyu Zhen in China is the largest electronic-waste dump in the world. Around a hundred truckloads of electronic trash arrive here every day to be sorted through by e-waste workers.

POLLUTION HOT SPOTS

Linfen isn't the only pollution hot spot. Here are some more examples.

Cubatão, Brazil, once had pollution like Linfen, but it is now much improved!

Let's get to work!

Making it better

- Cubatão, Brazil, is becoming a success story that Linfen might follow. It was once called the "Valley of Death" because of its terrible industrial pollution, which killed all of the trees and birds and poisoned the rivers. Local people have worked hard to clean it up, and it is no longer so bad.

- In many world locations, homes and factories are now being built with eco-friendly features. Eco-buildings use as little energy and create as little pollution as possible.

- Masdar City, in Abu Dhabi, United Arab Emirates, is being built as the world's first carbon-neutral city. Its buildings will all use renewable energy and the latest antipollution technologies.

07

The most haunted houses, ghoulish ghost towns, mysterious monuments, creepiest castles, scariest ships, spookiest celebrations, and spine-tingling skeletons. It's . . .

FRIGHT NIGHT

Mummies from the catacombs of Palermo, p. 130

BERMUDA TRIANGLE
& Other Spooky Seas

Can airplanes and ships mysteriously disappear at sea, with no explanation? It seems to depend on where they travel . . .

A TERRIBLE TALE

In 1945 five US Navy Avenger aircraft set out from Fort Lauderdale, Florida, on a routine training flight. The mission, known as Flight 19, was carrying 14 airmen. They never returned. That night the Navy sent more planes to search for the missing crew, but one of the rescue planes was seen exploding in midair. Where did this tragedy take place? It happened in the Bermuda Triangle.

TRIANGLE OF DOOM?

The fate of Flight 19 is among many strange disappearances of planes and boats reported in and around the famous Bermuda Triangle. It's an area of the Atlantic Ocean between Florida and the islands of Bermuda and Puerto Rico.

WHAT'S GOING ON?

Some say that the Bermuda Triangle is haunted by ancient spirits or even frequented by aliens. Others think that toxic gas bubbling up from the seabed might be sinking ships and confusing pilots. Nobody knows the truth.

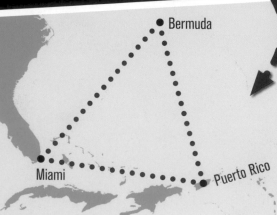

Bermuda

Miami

Puerto Rico

The Bermuda Triangle area

UNLUCKY LAKE

The Michigan Triangle is another scary-sounding watery spot, this time in Lake Michigan. Some say that when sailing or flying through it, time seems to stand still. Ship's captain George Donner was found to have vanished from his locked cabin in 1937, and a plane carrying 55 passengers disappeared suddenly in the area in 1955.

The spooky **Sargasso Sea** is a spot in the North Atlantic where ocean currents create a still, eerily calm area filled with thick seaweed. Boats can get stuck there because of the lack of wind, and legends tell of empty ships found floating, abandoned by their crew.

Since the 1990s, more than a dozen planes have mysteriously crashed near the islands of **Los Roques,** off Venezuela.

Old sailors' tales said that the Sargasso Sea's seaweed (shown below) could entangle ships and even eat people!

WORRYING WATERS

The Bermuda Triangle isn't the only stretch of water that's said to swallow up planes, boats, and sailors without a trace . . .

Welcome to my ghostly galleon? I may have sunk, but I won't stop sailing?

THE SHIPWRECK THAT WON'T SHUT UP

Australia has its own spooked sea spot. The cargo ship *Alkimos* (left) foundered off the coast in 1963, and the wreck is famous for haunting happenings. These include footsteps, smells of cooking, and a ghost wearing a seaman's coat and rubber boots, nicknamed "Harry."

Tower
of London

The Tower of London is almost 1,000 years old, and a number of English monarchs have used it as their very own private prison. Some of its prisoners took a one-way trip to the execution block and are now said to haunt its creepy courtyards and ancient stone passageways.

MY HOBBY IS CHOPPING!

HENRY'S HORRIBLE HABIT

Bloodthirsty English king Henry VIII (left), who reigned from 1508 to 1547, made a habit of sending enemies to the Tower and ordering their beheading. The most aristocratic prisoners were executed inside the Tower precincts, away from crowds. Others were executed publicly on nearby Tower Hill.

POOR LITTLE PRINCES

The Tower's most famous residents were two young princes, Edward and Richard, ages 12 and 9. Edward became king in 1483, but the boys' uncle Richard sent them to live in the Tower and seized the throne for himself, becoming Richard III. The princes disappeared and were said to have been murdered. Guards have reported seeing their ghosts floating around, dressed in nightshirts and holding hands.

HENRY'S HEADLESS EX

Henry VIII's second wife, Anne Boleyn, was beheaded at the Tower. Henry was annoyed that she didn't provide him with a son and accused her of being unfaithful to him. Anne had her head cut off in the Tower precincts, and her ghost is said to wander around carrying her head under her arm.

WHERE SHALL I PUT MY HAT?

WOW FACTOR

IN 1674 REMODELING WORKERS FOUND TWO CHILDREN'S SKELETONS HIDDEN UNDER A STAIRCASE IN THE TOWER. NOBODY KNOWS WHETHER THEY WERE THE LOST TOWER PRINCES.

MORE TOWER GHOSTS

- Legend has it that Margaret Pole, the Countess of Salisbury, refused to bend down to have her head chopped off, as ordered by Henry VIII. The executioner chased her and swiped at her with his ax to kill her. The ghastly scene is said to reappear in ghostly form.

- After being queen for just nine days in 1553, Lady Jane Grey was forced from power and ended up being executed in the Tower. She is said to appear on the turrets in a white gown.

- The Tower once housed a royal zoo, and in 1815 a sentry at the Tower saw a giant bear rushing toward him, centuries after the zoo had closed. He tried to stab it with his bayonet, but he passed right through it. Legend has it that he died of fright.

DAY OF THE DEAD

A spook-based celebration takes place in Mexico on November 1 and 2 every year. It's called Día de los Muertos, or the Day of the Dead (though it's actually two days). If you're in Mexico around this time, you'll see skeletons and skulls decorating cemeteries, houses, schools, and stores.

WELCOMING THE DEAD

The Day of the Dead is a festival for remembering those who have died. People make special shrines and offerings for the dead in the belief that, just for a day or two, the dead are able to visit Earth again and be close to their loved ones. The Day of the Dead may sound scary, but it is actually great fun!

People have parties and parades (right) and make up songs about the friends and relatives who are no longer with them.

SMART SKELETON

The Catrina (below) is a type of doll used as decoration during the Day of the Dead. It represents a skeleton lady dressed in fine clothes. People also dress up as a Catrina for parades.

What to do on the Day of the Dead
During the festival people might . . .

● . . . visit cemeteries and graves to clean them and decorate them with special *ofrendas* (offerings for the dead). Offerings include candles, toys, sugar skulls, flowers, drinks, and skeleton dolls.

● . . . make a shrine at home, filled with offerings and festival foods.

● . . . go to parties, dances, or parades wearing skeleton costumes and face paint. It is traditional to make a lot of music and noise as a way to wake up the dead.

● . . . make beds out of pillows and blankets for the dead to rest on when they visit.

BREAD OF THE DEAD

Any Day of the Dead feast must include *pan de muerto*, or "bread of the dead." This sweet cakelike bread is shaped into skulls or round loaves decorated with bone shapes.

FLOWER OF THE DEAD

Orange marigolds are used to decorate graves and shrines. The bright color is said to act as a beacon to show dead spirits the way home.

PALERMO'S CREEPY CATACOMBS

If you ever visit Palermo, Italy, you could go to one of the world's weirdest attractions—a vast underground collection of dried-out dead people dressed to look just like they did when they were alive. Is this the planet's most terrifying tourist place?

BROTHERS BELOW

The catacombs of Palermo are underground burial chambers built around 400 years ago underneath the city's Capuchin monastery, after the monks who lived and died there ran out of space in their graveyard. The first monk to be laid to rest in the chambers was Brother Silvestro of Gubbio. He is still there to welcome visitors at the entrance.

DRY AS A BONE

The underground rocks in this area of Italy are very good at soaking up moisture, and the monks found that any body left underground soon dried out. Instead of rotting, the bodies could be stuffed, dried, and preserved as mummies. Although some of the mummies have fallen apart and are now just skeletons, others still have their skin, hair, and eyes. They are often arranged in lifelike poses and seem to be looking around or having conversations.

I'd shake hands but I don't have any!

DEAD DECORATION

The Sedlec Ossuary, also called the "Bone Church," could perhaps beat Palermo's catacombs as the world champion of creepy creations. In medieval times, people clamored to be buried at this church in the Czech Republic because it was thought to be on especially holy ground. In 1870 the skeletons stored in the basement—at least 40,000 of them—were arranged into amazing patterns and decorations, including a stunning bone chandelier.

WHO'S WHO?

The Palermo bodies are arranged along the walls of long halls and passageways, divided into different areas for different types of people. There are male and female sections, as well as areas for children, priests, doctors, lawyers, and teachers, dressed in the clothes they wore in life.

OOH!

WOW FACTOR

THE SEDLEC CHANDELIER CONTAINS AT LEAST ONE EXAMPLE OF EVERY BONE IN THE HUMAN BODY.

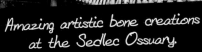
Amazing artistic bone creations at the Sedlec Ossuary.

DRESSED IN THEIR BEST

The people who were buried in the catacombs were usually wealthy and well dressed, and they didn't want that to stop when they died. You can see many of the mummies dressed in their nicest outfits, some with fancy hats, bonnets, jewelry, or umbrellas.

Lizzie Borden's
HAUNTED HOUSE

Wooooooooo! Knock . . . knock . . . For a truly frightful night, you could stay in a haunted house. One of the most notorious of all was the scene of a terrible murder and is now a hotel.

HOUSE OF HORROR

Lizzie Borden's house in Fall River, Massachusetts (right), was the location of a shocking murder in 1892. Andrew Borden and his wife, Abby, were found hacked to death with an ax, and their 22-year-old daughter Lizzie was accused of the crime. There was a famous song about the case (below).

Lizzie Borden

Lizzie Borden took an ax
and gave her father 40 whacks.
When she saw what she had done,
she gave her mother 41! "

In fact, Andrew Borden died from 11 whacks of the ax, and his wife was found with 19. Though many people think Lizzie Borden was the killer, she was actually found not guilty and freed.

SPOOKY SLEEP

To this day nobody knows who murdered the Bordens, but their house is famous for spooky goings-on. It is now a bed-and-breakfast hotel, and some staff and guests have reported seeing ghostly women in 19th-century clothes, doors opening by themselves, and bed coverings moving on their own. Others have heard whispered conversations, weeping, and footsteps.

PALACE OF GHOSTS

The palace of Hampton Court (right), near London, England, rivals Lizzie Borden's house for world-famous hauntings. It was once home to several kings and queens, some of whom seem to have stayed on. Catherine Howard, Henry VIII's fifth wife, was held captive here and, according to legend, she escaped and ran screaming down a hall. Visitors have reported hearing her cries and the sound of thumping on a door. Henry VIII himself is also said to wander the palace, and a nurse who once took care of his son Edward has supposedly been heard spinning on a spectral spinning wheel.

FAKE OR FRIGHT?

Something VERY scary was caught on closed-circuit television cameras at Hampton Court in 2003. A bizarre skeletal figure in a long cloak, swiftly nicknamed "Skeletor," appeared to come out of a castle door. Some people think it could be proof that ghosts exist. Others think it was a clever hoax.

Woof!

WOW FACTOR

WHEN FRANKLIN D. ROOSEVELT LIVED IN THE WHITE HOUSE IN THE 1940S, HIS DOG FALA WOULD OFTEN BARK AT SOMETHING INVISIBLE. WAS IT A GHOST, PERHAPS?

Lizzie Borden's House

WHITE HOUSE WANDERERS

The White House in Washington, DC, is the home of the president of the United States. Some presidents from the past liked it so much that it seems they never left! The most famous is President Abraham Lincoln, who died in 1865 when he was shot by an assassin. His ghost apparently appears sitting on a bed, pulling his boots on. Besides President Lincoln, other White House ghosts are said to include Lincoln's son Willie, at least four other presidents, and a spooky soldier.

GHOSTS OF CHERNOBYL

Why would an entire population suddenly abandon their homes, leaving an eerily empty ghost location? It has happened several times for various scary reasons, most famously at Chernobyl.

AWFUL EXPLOSION

When the nuclear power plant (right) in Chernobyl, Ukraine, exploded in 1986, deadly radiation meant that it wasn't safe to stay anywhere nearby. The town of Pripyat, built for workers at the power plant, was home to nearly 50,000 people, but they all had to leave and never returned. The poisoned ghost town is now collapsing and overrun with trees.

Geiger counters register high radiation at Pripyat.

Furniture and belongings are scattered in Pripyat's buildings, such as this old school.

Pripyat's lonely, abandoned Ferris wheel is one of its best-known landmarks.

LOST RESORT

Like Pripyat, Varosha in Cyprus stands abandoned by its population (right). It was once a top tourist destination, but in 1974, when Turkey invaded Cyprus, Varosha was taken over and closed off. Its inhabitants fled, and no one has ever been back to resettle it. Visitors have described how 40-year-old laundry still hangs on clotheslines. Old beach umbrellas still stand in front of deserted hotels, and stores are stocked with decaying 1970s products.

CURSED BY A DRAGON

This village of futuristic pod houses was built in the 1970s in Sanzhi, Taiwan. When several people died during the construction work, the project was abandoned. Some said that it was cursed because a Chinese dragon sculpture had been damaged to make way for a road to the houses. After years as a sightseeing destination and movie backdrop, the whole place was demolished.

READY, SETS, GO!

Being empty, Craco makes a good filming location. It appeared in the James Bond movie *Quantum of Solace.*

CREEPY CRACO

On a steep hilltop in southern Italy, the wind whistles through the empty streets and stone archways of Craco, abandoned in 1963. The ancient village has stood for more than 1,000 years but, thanks to a series of earthquakes and landslides, things got so dangerous that everyone was moved out. You can still visit Craco and experience its spooky silences for yourself.

STRANGE HAUNTED PLACES

It's not just creaky old houses and castles that are haunted. There are all kinds of other strange locations, indoors and out, that are said to have their own ghosts and ghouls.

SPOOKY STONES

According to legend, the ancient Rollright Stones in Oxfordshire, England (right), were once a troop of royal knights who were turned to stone by a witch. She did the same to their king, who was turned into the biggest stone. It is said that the cursed knights come back to life at midnight and wander down to the river for a drink. Some claim the stones are impossible to count, and if you count them more than once, you will get different answers. Strangely, many people have found this to be true.

Me thirsty!

SPOOKY STAGE

Ghosts seem to like theaters and, instead of being scared, actors are happy to see them because they are supposed to bring good luck. One of the most haunted theaters of all is said to be the Theatre Royal, Drury Lane, in London, England (right), where many people claim to have spotted the same ghost, known as the Man in Grey. He appears in 18th-century clothes, with a dressy hat and sword. He is said to be the ghost of someone whose skeleton was discovered in a walled-up and forgotten theater passage in 1848. It had a knife in its ribs.

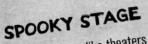

THEATRE ROYAL DRURY LANE

A CREEPY CROWD
Other Drury Lane ghosts are said to include . . .

- A clown ghost called Grimaldi (left), who is said to guide nervous actors onto the stage.
- The bad-tempered ghost of an actor who once murdered another actor in the theater during an argument.
- The ghost of monarch Charles II, along with some ghostly partying companions.
- A ghost who sits in the audience.
- The ghost of a dead comedian who long ago had his last laugh.

Web link
See pictures of ghosts in the Willard library: www.willardghost.com

HAIRY DRIVING

Even roads are said to be haunted. One is the country road between Postbridge and Two Bridges in Devon, England. In the early 1900s it was the scene of many strange road accidents. Drivers said that they had felt, and sometimes seen, a huge, strong pair of hairy hands grabbing their steering wheel.

LADY IN THE LIBRARY

The Willard Library (above) in Evansville, Indiana, is home to a ghost called the Grey Lady. She's said to be a quiet, kind-looking old lady who appears briefly, often in the children's section. She's become so famous that the library holds ghost tours and has webcams set up to try to spot her.

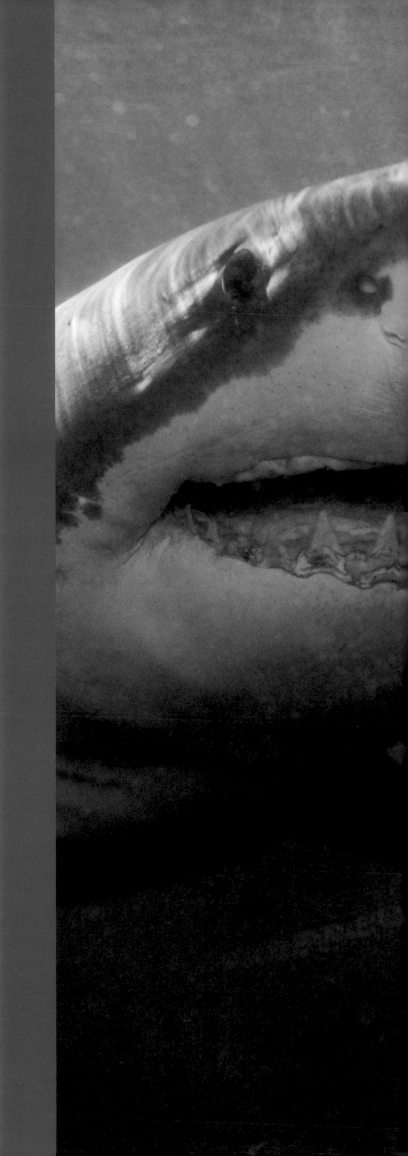

The scariest, most dangerous, hottest, coldest, most bug-filled, swampiest, stormiest, strangest, most unpredictable, and most explosive . . .

DANGEROUS PLACES

Worst shark bite spots, p. 142

SOUTHERN OCEAN PERIL

Giant waves, howling winds, icebergs, and deadly currents can make the oceans the deadliest spots on Earth. The scariest one of all is the Southern Ocean.

SCARY DOWN SOUTH

Of all the world's oceans, the Southern Ocean (right) is the deadliest and most feared by sailors. It runs all the way around Antarctica and, being close to the South Pole, it's f-f-f-FREEZING cold!

WILD AND WINDY

With very little land to get in the way, winds in the Southern Ocean roar around and around the planet, picking up fearsome speed. The ocean lies in the latitudes of 40°–70° South and, because of the eye-watering winds, seafarers have named these latitudes the Roaring Forties, Furious Fifties, and Screaming Sixties.

Southern Ocean waves can reach 60 ft. (18.2 m) or more, overwhelming ships.

AWESOME WAVES

A big wave breaking on the shore can be a deadly killer. That doesn't stop some thrill-seeking surfers, who travel the world in search of the biggest breakers to ride.

• In Nazaré, Portugal, in 2013 surfer Garrett McNamara caught what's thought to be the biggest wave ever ridden—it was around 100 ft. (30 m) high.

• Even bigger surfing waves sometimes form at Pe'ahi in Hawaii (left). They are so dangerous that the beach there has been nicknamed "Jaws."

WOW FACTOR

THE BIGGEST ICEBERG ON RECORD, NAMED B-15, MEASURED ALMOST 190 MI. (300 KM) LONG WHEN IT FIRST APPEARED IN 2000.

WHIRLED TO DOOM

Could a giant whirlpool suck in a ship? There are actually very few large whirlpools. They include Moskstraumen and Saltstraumen in Norway, Old Sow in Canada, Naruto in Japan (shown below) and Corryvreckan in Scotland. In all of these places, water whirls into a spiral as the tide flows through narrow channels. Big ships are safe, but whirlpools have sunk smaller boats and are very dangerous for swimmers.

ICEBERG!

Icebergs are always a danger around the Arctic and Antarctica (above), but large ones can float a long way before they melt, and some even come close to the equator. They are big, heavy, and unpredictable and can suddenly roll over, crushing or swamping boats. Ninety percent of the ice is below the surface, so it's easy for a ship to crash into the hidden underwater part. In 1912 the *Titanic*, one of the biggest, strongest ships ever built at the time, sank when it hit an iceberg at night in the North Atlantic Ocean. More than 2,000 people died.

BIG BITES
IN NEW SMYRNA

Where are you most likely to meet a marauding monster that could bite? Check out parts of the world where you might become a snack for a shark or a crocodile or even get mercilessly munched by a hippo.

SHARK CENTRAL

Sharks aren't as dangerous as most people think. They kill fewer people each year than crocodiles, dogs, or even bees. Florida's New Smyrna Beach is the top spot in the United States for shark attacks. In fact, it has so many incidents that it is often said to be the world shark bite capital.

Swim faster, fish food!

WHY NEW SMYRNA?

Surfers love New Smyrna for its waves, but they share the ocean with sharks that come into Ponce Inlet, an area where a river joins the ocean and there is a bumper haul of fish to eat.

TIGER TERRITORY

Tiger attacks are even rarer than shark bites, but not in the Sundarbans, a swampy, forested coastal area in India and Bangladesh. The Bengal tigers there (shown right) seem especially to like hunting humans and regularly come out of the forest to attack local fishermen and villagers.

GOBBLING GUSTAVE

African Nile crocodiles beat sharks as watery killers. They kill many people in the Nile and Congo rivers, even dragging their victims from boats. Locals blame a giant crocodile named Gustave for many deaths around Lake Tanzania in Burundi. Experts tried to catch him in 2002 but failed.

SORRY, WRONG SNACK!

New Smyrna's waters are cloudy, and it's thought that the sharks there tend to mistake surfers for prey such as seals. Most Smyrna shark bites aren't fatal. Usually a shark takes a nibble, realizes its mistake, and swims away.

DEADLY DELTA

Hippopotamuses are the most dangerous of all big biting animals, with huge chomping jaws that can easily bite a person in half. They are a danger all over Africa but especially in the Okavango delta in Botswana. The water there is shallow and often dries out, so hippos defend their area of water fiercely.

MORE SHARK SPOTS

- **Brazilian biting:** The Brazilian beach of Recife is plagued by killer bull sharks that like to munch on swimmers and surfers.

- **Danger down under:** Australia's east coast is home to many large shark species. Result? Regular deadly shark bites.

- **Shark picnic:** In Capetown, South Africa, there are many cage-diving tours that enable tourists to see sharks up close underwater. Food is put out to attract the sharks, luring many to the area. Swimmers beware!

Barrier Reef Beasties

Its beautiful, tropical blue waters are stuffed with amazing wildlife, so tourists flock to Australia's Great Barrier Reef to go snorkeling and diving among the coral. But they'd better watch out, because this is probably the world's number-one hot spot for dangerous sea creatures.

LUCKY ESCAPE!

In 2010 ten-year-old Rachel Shardlow was stung by a box jellyfish near the Great Barrier Reef. The stings covered her legs and would have killed most people, so doctors were amazed when Rachel recovered and was left with only scars.

BOX JELLYFISH

This killer jellyfish is box-shaped and see-through, with long, trailing tentacles.

DEADLY EFFECTS: The agonizingly painful sting stops the heart and lungs from working.

STAY SAFE: There are nets around some beaches to keep jellyfish out, and you can wear a jellyfish-sting-proof "stinger suit." If you're stung, pouring vinegar on the sting can help while you wait for an ambulance.

CONE SNAIL

The cone snail's beautiful shell means people often pick it up to look at it. Then–ZAP! The snail shoots out a dart that injects venom into the skin.

DEADLY EFFECTS: The sting knocks you out and can be fatal.

STAY SAFE: Never touch cone snail shells in case there's still something alive inside.

REEF STONEFISH

A knobbly, warty, speckled fish that is perfectly camouflaged on the seabed, the reef stonefish has thirteen venomous spines that will sting you if you step on it.

DEADLY EFFECTS: The venom can kill, but more often it's just mind-bogglingly painful.

STAY SAFE: Barrier Reef visitors should wear shoes when wading.

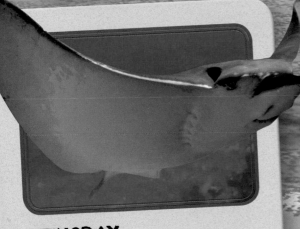

STINGRAY

The Great Barrier Reef has many species of stingrays–large flat fish with wide fins and a long tail that has a sharp, stinging spine on it.

DEADLY EFFECTS: A stingray can flick its stinger up suddenly to inject dangerous venom that is occasionally deadly.

STAY SAFE: Avoid stingrays' tails and don't approach them from behind.

BLUE-RINGED OCTOPUS

This tiny octopus, no bigger than your hand, has a horribly deadly bite. Its brown bumpy skin gives it camouflage, but when it is annoyed, it turns yellow with flashing blue rings.

DEADLY EFFECTS: The octopus's venom would paralyze you and stop you from breathing.

STAY SAFE: Never pick up this octopus. Anyone bitten must get to the hospital fast.

WOW FACTOR

THE GREAT BARRIER REEF HAS MANY FANTASTIC CREATURES THAT DON'T BITE OR STING. FOR INSTANCE, IT HAS THIRTY SPECIES OF WHALES, DOLPHINS, AND PORPOISES AND SIX SPECIES OF SEA TURTLES.

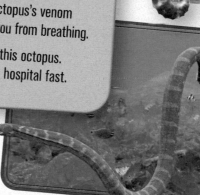

BEAKED SEA SNAKE

Most sea snakes are shy and timid, but the beaked sea snake is grumpy and aggressive and will bite people who disturb it as it swims in shallow water.

DEADLY EFFECTS: Its venom is so strong that one snake could kill 50 people!

STAY SAFE: Swimmers need to stay away from muddy river mouths where snakes lurk.

SUDDEN SINKHOLES

Some locations may seem harmless and peaceful when they're actually hiding scary secrets …

HORRIBLE HOLES

Is the ground beneath your feet solid? In Guatemala in Central America not one but two huge holes called sinkholes have suddenly opened up in the ground—one in 2007 and one in 2010 (shown right). They were caused by underground water washing away mud and sand so that the ground surface suddenly caved in. The terrifying sinkholes measured around 300 ft. (100 m) deep and 65 ft. (20 m) across.

KILLER QUICKSANDS

In movies quicksand slurps and squelches as it sucks its helpless victims down (left), but in reality sinking deep into quicksand is rare, though quicksand near Lake Okeechobee in Florida really did swallow an unlucky hiker whole in 1964. If you lie down on quicksand, you can float and wriggle to safety. The real danger comes if someone gets their feet stuck in quicksand on a beach when the tide is coming in quickly. Quicksand locations in Turnagain, Alaska, and Morecambe Bay in England have trapped and drowned several victims who were stuck in sand and then caught by the fast-moving rising tides.

LAKE OF DEATH

Hidden danger can rise up from down below. For instance, in 1986 a cloud of suffocating gas descended on the villages around Lake Nyos in Cameroon, killing people and animals (left). The gas was natural carbon dioxide that had bubbled up from deep inside the volcanic lake's waters. Because the gas was heavier than air, it flowed down into the valleys, making it impossible to breathe.

PIPE PREVENTION

The serious and scary disaster at Lake Nyos was a "lake overturn," which happens when gas dissolved in a lake suddenly escapes. Overturns are very rare, but there are other lakes in central Africa that could one day do the same. Scientists are trying to prevent lake overturns by putting pipes in these lakes to channel the gas out safely.

SINKHOLE SPOTS

▶ In 2010 eight big sinkholes appeared around China in two weeks, creating road chaos. They may have been caused by earthquake activity.

▶ Coastal Florida is a top sinkhole spot because of water erosion. In 2013 a Florida man disappeared forever, presumed dead, when a sinkhole opened under his bedroom.

▶ In Tahala, Estonia, there are many sinkholes. One of them, nicknamed the "Witch's Well," sometimes miraculously fills up with water (probably from underground rivers).

THAT SINKING FEELING

In the famous Sherlock Holmes mystery *The Hound of the Baskervilles*, evil villain Jack Stapleton meets a sticky end when he sinks into the deadly Grimpen Mire. This fictional swamp was probably based on Fox Tor Mires in Devon, England (above). It's a scary swamp full of deep, peaty pools, made even more dangerous by the thick mists that sometimes gather there.

It's COLD at the POLES

The North and South poles are deadly locations, as explorers have discovered. If you stepped outside in the winter without warm clothing on, you would soon be as frozen as an icicle.

FATEFUL JOURNEYS

Early explorers first started trying to trek across Antarctica to reach the South Pole in 1901. They soon found that the ice fields, blizzards, high winds, steep mountains, slippery glaciers, and deadly cold made this extremely treacherous, and two expeditions had to turn back.

ATTEMPT ONE

Robert Scott (below) led the first expedition in 1901–1904 but gave up 410 mi. (660 km) from the South Pole.

ATTEMPT TWO

Ernest Shackleton (below, second left) led his own attempt in 1907–1909. He came within 112 mi. (180 km) of the South Pole but had to retreat to avoid an icy death. He said to his wife, "I thought, dear, that you would rather have a live ass than a dead lion!"

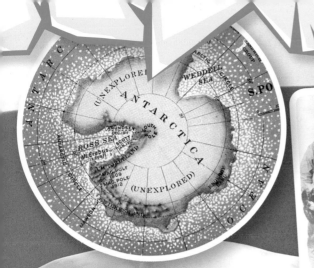

POLAR DANGERS

★ **Frostbite:** If body parts such as fingers, toes, and noses get too cold, they can freeze solid, turn black, and eventually fall off. When people go outside at the poles, they must keep their skin covered at all times to prevent frostbite.

★ **Whiteouts:** These polar snow blizzards are so thick that they make everything look white. You can't see where you are or find your way, and you could quickly get lost.

★ **Crevasses:** A crevasse is a deep crack in a glacier or ice sheet (shown left). Wide, gaping, slippery-sided crevasses have claimed many lives at the poles.

Robert Scott and his team died of cold.

Norwegian Roald Amundsen reached the South Pole.

THIRD TIME (UN)LUCKY:

Eventually, two expeditions in 1910–1912 made it to the South Pole. One was led by Norwegian Roald Amundsen, who reached the pole first and returned safely. The other was led by Robert Scott. After making it to the pole and finding that Amundsen had gotten there first, he and his men were caught in a blizzard, ran out of food, and froze to death in their tent.

DEEP-FROZEN EXPLORERS

Captain Scott (left) and three men were eventually found where they froze. One of the party, Captain Oates, had left the tent and walked off to his death in order to leave enough food for his friends. A cairn (monument of stones) was built near where he is thought to have perished. His body was never found.

NORTHERN PERIL

The frozen north of the world holds its own special dangers. Parts of the Arctic Ocean are permanently frozen over, but large areas freeze only during the winter. When the thaw comes, it is possible to get trapped on its dangerous ice floes, and there is the added danger of polar bears. These giant meat eaters have paws as big as dinner plates, with long claws. They have a great sense of smell and can run surprisingly fast, too.

SHAKE ZONES

Earthquakes can happen almost anywhere in the world. However, there are some top danger spots where the biggest and most dangerous quakes are likely to strike.

JIGSAW PUZZLE

Earth's surface is made up of huge, slowly moving sections or "plates" of rocky crust that fit together like the pieces of a giant jigsaw puzzle. The worst areas for earthquakes are around the edges of these sections, where one plate can suddenly slide or slip against another.

SHAKING SCALE

The Richter scale is a measurement of how much energy an earthquake releases. The scale ranges from 0 to around 10, with the biggest quakes on record measuring between 9 and 9.5. The quake is recorded on a seismograph (below).

WHAT TO DO IF IT HAPPENS TO YOU

If you're ever caught in an earthquake . . .

1. Shelter under strong furniture or in a doorway.

2. If you're outside, move away from buildings.

3. Don't assume it's over. There may be more tremors!

RING OF FIRE

The plates under the Pacific Ocean are especially likely to cause earthquakes and volcanic activity. Because of this, the coast around the Pacific is a danger zone known as the Ring of Fire. It includes these major earthquake locations:

- **Alaska:** A huge magnitude 9.2 earthquake struck here in 1964.
- **California:** Several deadly quakes have shaken the California coast, such as the San Francisco earthquake of 1906 and the Loma Prieta quake in 1989.
- **Chile:** Location of the most powerful quake on record, the Great Chilean Earthquake of 1960, measuring 9.5 on the Richter scale.
- **Japan:** A major earthquake hot spot, Japan's quakes include the Kobe earthquake of 1995 and the 2011 Tohoku quake, which led to a killer tsunami that claimed more than 15,000 lives.
- **New Zealand:** This island nation lies right on the Ring of Fire and suffers serious earthquakes, such as the Christchurch quake of 2011.

OUTSIDE THE RING

Besides the Ring of Fire, there are plenty of other plate boundaries and earthquake danger zones. For instance, Iran has been plagued by serious earthquakes since ancient times. The Caribbean islands can suffer terrible quakes, such as the devastating Haiti earthquake of 2010 (above). China was the location of the deadliest earthquake on record, the Shaanxi earthquake of 1556, in which there was great loss of life.

A giant crack in the road caused by an earthquake in Haiti in 2010.

QUAKES AND TSUNAMIS

Earthquakes under the sea can make large sections of seabed shift around. This causes huge ripples on the sea surface, which spread out across the ocean. When they reach land, they rise up into huge waves called tsunamis.

POMPEII:

THE BURIED CITY

In southern Italy, near the city of Naples, there stands an ancient Roman ghost town called Pompeii. You can visit it and see the old stores, temples, and homes, along with preserved everyday objects such as plates and even loaves of bread. But there's something more chilling here—the plaster casts of dead people caught at the moment their lives ended.

DEATH ERUPTS

Towering over Pompeii is Mount Vesuvius, one of the world's most dangerous and explosive volcanoes. Almost 2,000 years ago, in AD 79, an enormous eruption covered Pompeii and nearby villages in a deep layer of rock, ash, and burning gas. Though some people managed to get away, thousands were trapped and buried alive.

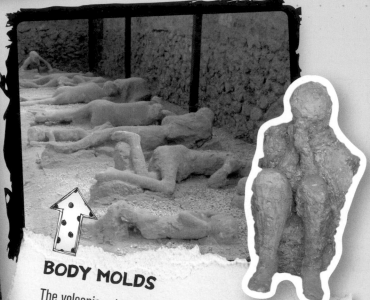

BODY MOLDS

The volcanic ash hardened where it fell, leaving hollows where the bodies of the victims once were. These hollow shapes have since been used to make plaster-cast models of the victims (shown above).

Ruins of Pompeii

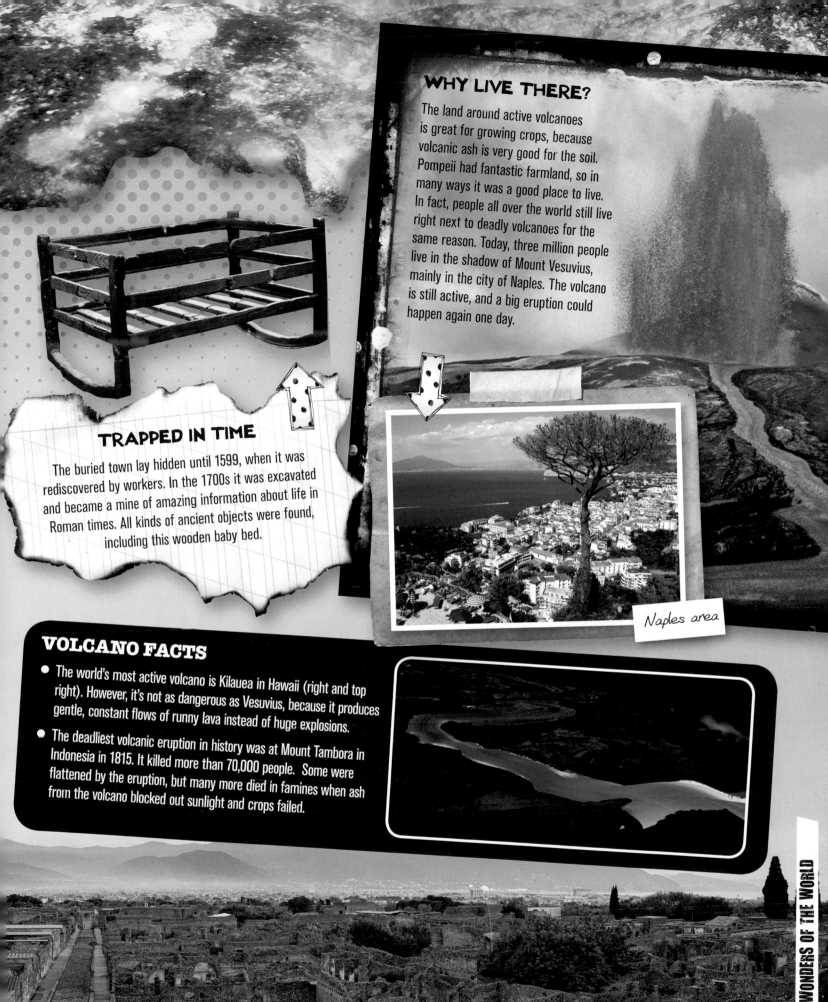

WHY LIVE THERE?

The land around active volcanoes is great for growing crops, because volcanic ash is very good for the soil. Pompeii had fantastic farmland, so in many ways it was a good place to live. In fact, people all over the world still live right next to deadly volcanoes for the same reason. Today, three million people live in the shadow of Mount Vesuvius, mainly in the city of Naples. The volcano is still active, and a big eruption could happen again one day.

TRAPPED IN TIME

The buried town lay hidden until 1599, when it was rediscovered by workers. In the 1700s it was excavated and became a mine of amazing information about life in Roman times. All kinds of ancient objects were found, including this wooden baby bed.

Naples area

VOLCANO FACTS

- The world's most active volcano is Kilauea in Hawaii (right and top right). However, it's not as dangerous as Vesuvius, because it produces gentle, constant flows of runny lava instead of huge explosions.

- The deadliest volcanic eruption in history was at Mount Tambora in Indonesia in 1815. It killed more than 70,000 people. Some were flattened by the eruption, but many more died in famines when ash from the volcano blocked out sunlight and crops failed.

DEATH VALLEY: THE DEADLY DESERT

Deep in the Mojave Desert in California lies one of the most famously deadly destinations of them all—the scary-sounding Death Valley. It's a fascinating but fearsome place to visit, and to stay safe there you need to know what you're doing.

HORRIBLY HOT

Death Valley holds the record for the hottest temperature ever measured on Earth—a thermometer-busting 134°F (56.7°C), recorded in the summer of 1913. It's also the lowest place anywhere in the United States. Even though the bottom of Death Valley lies 282 ft. (86m) below sea level, it's very dry.

My home is hot!

IN THE OVEN

Why is Death Valley so hot? The deep valley is surrounded by high mountains, and very few rain clouds can reach it. With no cloud cover, the blazing sun heats up the air in the valley all day long. The air can't escape—it just swirls up and down, getting hotter and hotter, like the air inside an oven.

WHO LIVES HERE?

The deepest part of the valley is spookily named "Badwater Basin" (right) and is home to a rare but supertough survivor, the Badwater snail. These small snails lurk under the Basin's salty crust. They can survive high temperatures but not tourists' boots. If you ever visit Death Valley, be careful not to squash them!

WOW FACTOR

DEATH VALLEY DANGERS

If you still feel like a visit to Death Valley, these are the main dangers to watch out for:

- **Extreme heat:** High temperatures can soon lead to heatstroke for humans.

- **Dehydration:** There's no safe natural drinking water, so you have to bring a lot with you. The heat makes people VERY thirsty.

- **Extreme cold:** Yes, despite being so hot, Death Valley can also be very cold at night, when the temperature drops suddenly.

- **Flash floods:** There's very little rain in the valley–only about 2 in. (5 cm) a year–but it falls in sudden, heavy showers that can cause dangerous floods.

- **Rattlesnakes:** These venomous vipers hide from the sun's heat under rocks and in shady spots.

- **Mountain lions:** They're rare, but these big cats, also called cougars, have been known to attack people.

- **Mineshafts:** The valley is full of old mine tunnels and deep shafts that you could get lost in or fall down. Don't trip on the trip!

THE CLUE'S IN THE NAME

According to legend, Death Valley got its name during the great California gold rush of 1849. Thousands of people headed to the area to find gold, but some got lost and stumbled into the hostile valley on the way. As she left, one woman is said to have yelled, "Goodbye, death valley!" and the name stuck.

BAD BOTTOM

Badwater Basin (below) is muddy and filled with dried salt. There's a small pool of water that's undrinkable because of the salt dissolved in it. Sometimes, after a rainstorm, more water collects here, forming a temporary lake called Lake Badwater–but it soon dries up in the scorching sun.

INDEX

THE REAL WONDERS OF THE WORLD

1st Edition
Published September 2013

WELDONOWEN

Conceived by Weldon Owen in partnership with Lonely Planet
Produced by Weldon Owen, an imprint of
Red Lemon Press Limited
Northburgh House, 10 Northburgh Street
London EC1V 0AT, UK

Copyright © 2013 Weldon Owen Limited
www.redlemonpress.com

Red Lemon Press Limited is part of the Bonnier Publishing Group
www.bonnierpublishing.com

Project managed and commissioned by Dynamo Limited
Authors: Moira Butterfield, Anna Claybourne, and Tim Collins
Editor: Moira Butterfield
Design: Dynamo Limited

Published by
Lonely Planet Publications Pty. Ltd. ABN 36 005 607 983
90 Maribyrnong St, Footscray, Victoria 3011, Australia

ISBN 978-1-74321-734-4

A CIP catalogue record for this book is available from the British Library.

Printed and bound in China by 1010 Printing Int. Ltd.
9 8 7 6 5 4 3 2 1

MIX
Paper from responsible sources
FSC
www.fsc.org FSC® C021741

Paper in this book is certified against the Forest Stewardship Council™ standards. FSC™ promotes environmentally responsible, socially beneficial and economically viable management of the world's forests.

CREDITS

Key – tl top left, tc top center, tr top right, cl center left, c center, cr center right, bl bottom left, bc bottom center, br bottom right.

All images © Shutterstock except:

4tr, 19bl, 21br, 40tl, 40c, 44tr, 44b, 45cr, 45br, 46bl, 47tl, 47tr, 47bl, 50tl, 51tl (LEGOLAND® Billund Resort), 57br, 60bc, 61bl, 65br, 71cr, 72tr, 83bl, 83br, 88cl, 88bl, 88br, 91cl, 97tl, 105bl, 105br, 112c, 112cl, 112br, 113br, 125cr, 131tl, 135cl, 137tr, 145br, 151tr, 153cr, 57bl; 115tl **Alamy;** 1br, 4c, 15tl, 17 bc, 20r, 21tl, 23cl, 25tc, 26cr, 27tr, 30c, 32c, 32bl, 33tr, 33c, 33cr, 39tl, 39tr, 50c (LEGOLAND® Windsor Resort), 51cr, 52c, 55tl, 55cl, 55cr, 55bl, 56tr, 56cl, 56b, 57tc, 61tr, 61br, 62bl, 63br, 65cl, 71bl, 71br, 72bl, 73tl, 73tr, 73cl, 73cr, 75tr, 79br, 80c, 81br, 82c, 82bl, 87tl, 91cr, 92cl, 96tl, 96bl, 97bl, 98cl, 99tr, 99cl, 99br, 100c, 101cl, 102c, 104c, 106c, 107tl, 107cr, 107cl, 114c, 114bc, 115cr, 115br, 116c, 117tl, 117tr, 118c, 118bl, 122c, 124cr, 126bl, 127tr, 128c, 130bl, 131bl, 132c, 137tc, 138c, 140tr, 140bl, 141tl, 141cl, 142tl, 143tr, 143br, 144c, 145tl, 146c, 146bl, 147c, 147br, 148cl, 148bl, 148br, 149tc, 149tr, 149cl, 150c, 152cl, 152c, 152bc, 153tr, 154c, 155cl **Corbis;** 46c, 46tr **Courtesy of Chutters;** 64bc, 65tl, 65tr **Courtesy of Cirque de Soleil;** 52br **Courtesy of Formula Rossa;** 53br **Courtesy of Dream World;** 47cr **Courtesy of Papabubble;** 137br **Courtesy of Willard Library;** 7cl, 23cr, 36tl, 39bc, 42bl, 43cr, 43bl, 43br, 45tr, 47bl, 51tr, 53tl, 53tr, 53cl, 71bc, 76c, 77tl, 77br, 84c, 87c, 89br, 91br, 97cr, 120c, 121tl, 121tc, 121tr, 121cr, 125bl, 127cl, 129bl, 130bc, 132cr, 135tr, 136bl, 140br, 141c, 141br, 147tc, 148c, 150cl, 153tl, 153br, 154bl, 155br **Getty;** 7bl, 16 cr, 19tc, 19tr, 19cr, 24c, 24cl, 25cl, 33bl, 34cr, 35cr, 35bl, 59bc, 60c, 62tr, 62bc, 63cl, 87tr, 89tr, 98br, 100bl, 106b **Rex.**

Also available in the series

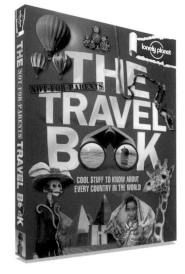
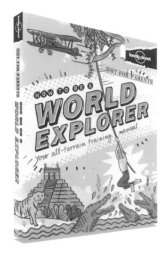

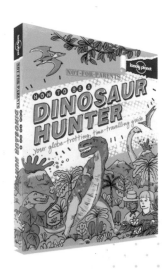

Everything You Ever Wanted to Know series

LONELY PLANET OFFICES

Australia Head Office
Locked Bag 1, Footscray, Victoria 3011
phone 03 8379 8000
fax 03 8379 8111

USA
150 Linden St., Oakland, CA 94607
phone 510 250 6400,
toll free 800 275 8555
fax 510 893 8572

UK
Media Centre, 201 Wood Lane,
London W12 7TQ
phone 020 8433 1333
fax 020 8702 0112